First World War
and Army of Occupation
War Diary
France, Belgium and Germany

7 DIVISION
Divisional Troops
10 Sanitary Section (2 London Sanitary Company)
1 August 1916 - 31 March 1917

WO95/1648/2

The Naval & Military Press Ltd
www.nmarchive.com
Published in association with The National Archives

Published by

The Naval & Military Press Ltd

Unit 10 Ridgewood Industrial Park,
Uckfield, East Sussex,
TN22 5QE England
Tel: +44 (0) 1825 749494

www.naval-military-press.com

www.nmarchive.com

This diary has been reprinted in facsimile from the original. Any imperfections are inevitably reproduced and the quality may fall short of modern type and cartographic standards.

© Crown Copyright
Images reproduced by permission of The National Archives, London, England, 2015.

Contents

Document type	Place/Title	Date From	Date To
Heading	WO95/1648/2		
Heading	7th Division No 10 Sanitary Section Formerly 2nd London Sanitary Coy 1916 Aug-1917 Mar		
Heading	Section 10 2nd London Sanitary Coy RAMC., T. 7th Division B.Y, Force France War Diary Vol 1 From 1 August 1916 To August 31st 1916		
War Diary	Picquigny	01/08/1916	12/08/1916
War Diary	Heilly	13/08/1916	13/08/1916
War Diary	Buire Sur-l-Ancre	14/08/1916	31/08/1916
Diagram etc	VII. Divnl Sanitary Arrangements		
Diagram etc	Disposal Of Excreta		
Diagram etc	Incinerators		
Diagram etc	Bath Houses		
Diagram etc	Bath Houses Ctd		
Heading	Section 10 2nd London Sanitary Coy RAMC., T Attached to 7th Division B.E. Force France War Diary Vol 2 From 1st September 1916 To 30th September 1916		
War Diary	Buire-Sur-L-Ancre	01/09/1916	10/09/1916
War Diary	Airaines	11/09/1916	12/09/1916
War Diary	Hallencourt	13/09/1916	18/09/1916
War Diary	Bailleul	19/09/1916	19/09/1916
War Diary	Fletre	20/09/1916	21/09/1916
War Diary	Pont De Neippe	22/09/1916	30/09/1916
Heading	Section 10 2nd London Sanitary Coy RAMC., T 7th Division B.E. Force. France 10th Sanitary Section War Diary Vol 3 From 1st October 1916 To 31st October 1916		
War Diary	Pont De Neippe	01/10/1916	31/10/1916
Heading	Section 2nd London Sanitary Coy R.A.M.C. T. 7th Division B.E.Force France War Diary Vol 4 From 1st November 1916 To 30th November 1916		
War Diary	Pont De Neippe	01/11/1916	04/11/1916
War Diary	Fletre	05/11/1916	09/11/1916
War Diary	Renescure	10/11/1916	11/11/1916
War Diary	Tilques	12/11/1916	15/11/1916
War Diary	Lumbres	16/11/1916	16/11/1916
War Diary	Bomy	17/11/1916	18/11/1916
War Diary	Anvin	19/11/1916	19/11/1916
War Diary	Flers	20/11/1916	20/11/1916
War Diary	Frohen Le Grand	21/11/1916	21/11/1916
War Diary	Doullens	22/11/1916	22/11/1916
War Diary	Marieux	23/11/1916	25/11/1916
War Diary	Bertrancourt	26/11/1916	30/11/1916
Heading	Section 10 2nd London Sanitary Coy. R.A.M.C. T. B.E.F. France War Diary Vol 5 1st December 1916 To 31st December 1916		
War Diary	Bertrancourt	01/12/1916	31/12/1916

Heading	No. 10 Section 2nd London Sanitary Coy. R.A.M.C. T B.E.F. France War Diary 1st January 1917-31st January 1917 Vol 6		
War Diary	Bertrancourt	01/01/1917	31/01/1917
Miscellaneous	D.D.M.S V Corps	04/03/1917	04/03/1917
Heading	No. 10 Section 10 2nd London Sanitary Coy R.A.M.C. T. B.E.F. France 7th Division War Diary From 1st Feb To 28th Feb 1917 Volume 7		
War Diary	Bertrancourt	01/02/1917	28/02/1917
Heading	No. 10 Section 2nd London Sanitary Coy R.A.M.C. T B.E. Force France War Diary From 1st March To 31st March 1917 Vol 8		
War Diary	Bertrancourt	01/03/1917	27/03/1917
War Diary	Miraumont	28/03/1917	31/03/1917

WO 95/1648/2

7TH DIVISION

No 10 SANITARY SECTION
formerly 2ND LONDON SANITARY COY.
~~AUG - DEC 1916~~
1916 AUG — 1917 MAR

To 1st ARMY

— CONFIDENTIAL —

Section 10.
2nd London Sanitary Coy., R.A.M.C., T.
7th Division
B.E. Force
France

— WAR DIARY —

(VOL. I.)

from August 1st 1916 to August 31st 1916

COMMITTEE FOR THE
MEDICAL HISTORY OF THE WAR
Date 26 OCT. 1916

WAR DIARY
or
INTELLIGENCE SUMMARY

(Erase heading not required.)

Army Form C. 2118.

Instructions regarding War Diaries and Intelligence Summaries are contained in F. S. Regs., Part II. and the Staff Manual respectively. Title Pages will be prepared in manuscript.

Place	Date	Hour	Summary of Events and Information	Remarks and references to Appendices
PICQUIGNY	1st to 11th August 1916		At PICQUIGNY having gone there on July 22nd the sanitation of the area occupied by the Division has been much improved. The health of the Division continues good. No 2413 Pte Shear, suffering from Dysentery, was notified on the 2nd in the 8th Corps, the case was investigated with a view to finding the source of infection the billet was disinfected & instructions given re-contacts. On the 1st inst. No 22951 Pte Spurgin, 2nd Royal Warwickshire Regt was notified as having Scarlet Fever. This man was desquamating when admitted to the Field Ambulance. He had just come from ROUEN a few days previously, he informed the Medical Officer of the 2nd Royal Warwicks that he had a slight rash on the ankles while at ROUEN. The billet was disinfected & contacts isolated. A careful enquiry amongst the civilian population in all the villages occupied by the Division was made for Infectious Diseases. None were found. All the units in the Division had the sanitary arrangements constructed on the system as indicated in the accompanying diagrams (sheets Nos 1 to 5 and 8. At PICQUIGNY where there was no available land	

2449 Wt. W14957/M90 750,000 1/16 J.B.C. & A. Forms/C.2118/12.

WAR DIARY
or
INTELLIGENCE SUMMARY
(Erase heading not required.)

Army Form C. 2118.

Place	Date	Hour	Summary of Events and Information	Remarks and references to Appendices
			for making latrines &c. the improved pail system of public latrines as indicated on drawings Nos 2 & 3 were made on suitable sites throughout the village and beside each latrine an incinerator as sketch 3 drawing No 2, was built, the contents of the pails were burnt with the refuse collected from the units occupying the village.

The various units of the Division except the 2nd Border Regiment & 1st South Staffordshire Regiment were inspected by the A.K.M.S. or D.A.D.M.S. I accompanied them on their rounds of inspection.

Bath houses on the "Hot spray" system were erected at PICQUIGNY and VAUX-en-Amienois. A bath house was also in use at HEILLY for the Artillery troops resting there. A Corporal of the Sanitary Section was in charge of each bath-house; 30 men from the 23rd Field Ambulance assisted at PICQUIGNY and 10 men from the 22nd Field Ambulance assisted at VAUX-en-Amienois. At the bath houses clean underclothing was issued to all troops and hot ironing of "service dress" was carried out; before ironing the seams were smeared with a solution of cresol and soap. During the time the Division was resting in this area 28,299 N.C.O's & men of the Division were bathed & clean underclothing given | |

WAR DIARY
or
INTELLIGENCE SUMMARY
(Erase heading not required.)

Army Form C. 2118.

Instructions regarding War Diaries and Intelligence Summaries are contained in F. S. Regs., Part II. and the Staff Manual respectively. Title Pages will be prepared in manuscript.

Place	Date	Hour	Summary of Events and Information	Remarks and references to Appendices
			A Disinfecting station was established at the bath-house at PICQUIGNY, & disinfection of was carried out in a Thresh steam disinfector mounted on a Foden steam lorry. All clothing was brought from the various bath-houses & passed through the Thresh's disinfector, it was then sorted and sent to the laundries at BOVES. The laundry at HEILLY was kept working during this time also, 30 women being employed to wash and repair the underclothing. The Corporal of the Sanitary Section in charge of the bath-house at HEILLY was also in charge of the laundry.	
			Service dress of units or of individual men that had become very verminous were passed through the Thresh steam disinfector while the men were having a bath. Blankets received from the Field Ambulances & units were also disinfected as were also the kits of the contacts of the cases of Infectious disease.	
			Infectious disease charts were brought up to date shewing positive cases occurring amongst Divisional troops during the month of July.	
			The motor lorry attached to the Section was employed each day in carrying clothing between PICQUIGNY and Vaux-en-Amiénois and	

WAR DIARY
or
INTELLIGENCE SUMMARY
(Erase heading not required.)

Army Form C. 2118.

Place	Date	Hour	Summary of Events and Information	Remarks and references to Appendices
			PICQUIGNY and the laundries at BOVES. No. 1255 Pte Hardcastle, 1st London Sanitary Co. R.A.M.C., T., joined the section as a reinforcement from No. 1 Territorial Base Depot, ROUEN on the 8th August 1916. On the 11th, I paraded with the Section for the inspection of the 20th Infantry Brigade by the IVth Army Commander. F.S. Carson, Capt. R.A.M.C.	
PICQUIGNY	12/8/16	2.30 a.m.	The Section set out from PICQUIGNY & marched to HANGEST-sur-SOMME, entrained at 5.30 a.m. and arrived at MERICOURT-L'ABBÉ at 10.30 a.m. where the section was detrained & marched to HEILLY. The lorry, attached to the section, with equipment, left PICQUIGNY at 10.30 a.m. & arrived at HEILLY at 1.30 p.m. Five Divisional lorries left PICQUIGNY at 2.30 p.m. with the clothing and equipment of the Division, arriving at HEILLY bath house at 5.30 p.m. The clothing and equipment was left in the stores at HEILLY and I reported at the A.D.M.S's office at RIBEMONT-sur-l'Abbé in the evening. The laundresses at HEILLY were paid to-day. F.S. Carson, Capt.	

WAR DIARY
or
INTELLIGENCE SUMMARY
(Erase heading not required.)

Army Form C. 2118.

Instructions regarding War Diaries and Intelligence Summaries are contained in F. S. Regs., Part II. and the Staff Manual respectively. Title Pages will be prepared in manuscript.

Place	Date	Hour	Summary of Events and Information	Remarks and references to Appendices
HEILLY	13/8/16		On instruction of the D.D.D.M.S. XVth Corps the Thresh steam disinfector on Foden lorry was sent to the IVth Army school at FLIXECOURT for the disinfection of clothing. One man from the Sanitary Section, in addition to the 2 drivers, was sent in charge. On instruction of the A.D.M.S. the Section & equipment moved to BUIRE-sur-l-Ancre to tents & bivouacs in a field. An orderly room was erected in the field at BUIRE-sur-l-Ancre occupied by the Section. № 10048 Pte W. Bradley of the 1st South Staffordshire Regiment, who was attached to the Sanitary Section was sent sick to the 23rd Field Ambulance. I visited bath houses at MEAULTE (E.18.a.9.0, Albert combined sheet) BUIRE-sur-l-Ancre (D.30.d.6.7 Albert combined sheet) and VILLE-sur-Ancre (E.26.a.2.6, Albert combined sheet): the first 2 were erected by the Division in January last. F.S. Cowan, Capt.	

2449 Wt. W14957/M90 750,000 1/16 J.B.C. & A. Forms/C.2118/12.

WAR DIARY
or
INTELLIGENCE SUMMARY
(Erase heading not required.)

Army Form C. 2118.

Instructions regarding War Diaries and Intelligence Summaries are contained in F. S. Regs., Part II. and the Staff Manual respectively. Title Pages will be prepared in manuscript.

Place	Date	Hour	Summary of Events and Information	Remarks and references to Appendices
BUIRE sur-l-Ancre	14/3/16		Area occupied by the Division divided & Inspectors allocated to each district. I reported to the A.D.M.S. and received instructions re-sanitation of the area occupied by the Division. — Reports have been received from several Medical Officers of Units, that the area occupied by them is dirty & in an insanitary condition. — The inspectors from the Sanitary Section have visited the various villages & camps occupied by the Division & reports of insanitary conditions have been received. The inspectors of the Section for the various areas allotted to them have sent in reports. — Advised the Town Major of BUIRE sur-l-Ancre re the sanitation of the village. The various villages occupied by the Division were visited and enquiries made re Infectious disease amongst the civilian population from the school teachers, Mayors & Curé's. Bath-houses at BUIRE-sur-l-Ancre (D 30 d 6.7 Albert combined sheet) and MEAULTE (E 16 a 9.0 Albert combined sheet) were cleaned out and made ready for bathing. F. S. Carson, Capt.	

WAR DIARY
or
INTELLIGENCE SUMMARY
(Erase heading not required.)

Army Form C. 2118.

Instructions regarding War Diaries and Intelligence Summaries are contained in F. S. Regs., Part II. and the Staff Manual respectively. Title Pages will be prepared in manuscript.

Place	Date	Hour	Summary of Events and Information	Remarks and references to Appendices
			The section lorry was employed in moving equipment & clothing to the bath-houses at BUIRE and MEAULTE and also obtaining timber for the bath-houses.	
			F S Cumon, Capt	
BUIRE sur-l-Ancre	13/7/16		Routine work in the sanitation of the various areas. Flies were very numerous in the whole area and horse manure heaps have been found in all the villages & camps, where troops have been billeted for some months Hot spray baths were fixed at BUIRE-sur-l-Ancre and MEAULTE and clean underclothing sent, from the stores at HEILLY to them. The arrangement of these 2 baths houses is shown on tracing N°7 attached hereto. An N.C.O. from the Sanitary Section has been put in charge at each bath-house and 7 men from the 23rd Field Ambulance have been sent to each bath-house. The Division has been notified that the bath houses are ready for bathing and programmes asked for.	

2449 Wt. W14957/M90 750,000 1/16 J.B.C. & A. Forms/C.2118/12.

WAR DIARY
or
INTELLIGENCE SUMMARY

Army Form C. 2118.

(Erase heading not required.)

Instructions regarding War Diaries and Intelligence Summaries are contained in F. S. Regs., Part II. and the Staff Manual respectively. Title Pages will be prepared in manuscript.

Place	Date	Hour	Summary of Events and Information	Remarks and references to Appendices
			An N.C.O. of the Section who was attached, temporarily, to the IX th Corps Headquarters to supervise the sanitation, rejoined the Section. The Sections lorry was employed in taking dirty underclothing and returning with clean, for the bath houses at BUIRE and MEAULTE. The Thresh steam disinfector on Foden lorry returned to H/Qt from FLIXECOURT. F. S. Cannon, Capt.	
BUIRE-sur-l'Ancre	16/8/16		On instruction from the A.D.M.S., I met Brig. General Steele of the 22nd Infantry Brigade at 9 a.m at DERNANCOURT and inspected the area occupied by the 22nd Infantry Brigade and advised on the insanitary conditions found. Five of the "PB" men attached to the Sanitary Section & stationed at RIBEMONT and one man from BUIRE were sent to DERNANCOURT to erect incinerators & deal with the insanitary conditions. Routine sanitation was carried on in the other areas. No 13629 Pte A Cowall, 2nd Royal Irish Regiment was reported on	

WAR DIARY
or
INTELLIGENCE SUMMARY

(Erase heading not required.)

Army Form C. 2118.

Instructions regarding War Diaries and Intelligence Summaries are contained in F. S. Regs., Part II. and the Staff Manual respectively. Title Pages will be prepared in manuscript.

Place	Date	Hour	Summary of Events and Information	Remarks and references to Appendices
			a case of suspected Enteric by the 23rd Field Ambulance, the cause of infection was investigated and instructions given re-contacts. No. 15786 Pte Sutton of the 9th Devons, was notified by the 23rd Field Ambulance, as a case of suspected Cerebro-Spinal-Meningitis - this case was investigated & instructions given re-contacts on whole billet was disinfected. Men of the 1st R Welsh Fusiliers were bathed at MEAULTE, 8th Devons at BUIRE and XVth Corps Adp troops & 7th Divisional Artillery at HEILLY, and clean underclothing was issued. The section lorry conveyed clothing to & from the laundries at BOVES. I reported at the ADMS's office at 6 p.m. F. S. Carson, Capt.	
BUIRE sur-l-Ancre	17/8/16		Routine sanitary duties were carried on by the sanitary section. Special attention has been given as to the destruction of fly larvae and flies, and the disposal of horse manure. On the advice of the	

2449 Wt. W14957/M90 750,000 1/16 J.B.C. & A. Forms/C.2118/12.

WAR DIARY or INTELLIGENCE SUMMARY

Army Form C. 2118.

(Erase heading not required.)

Place	Date	Hour	Summary of Events and Information	Remarks and references to Appendices
			A.D.M.S, units were instructed to cover fresh horse manure with earth. N.C.O.s and men of the 2nd Queens were bathed at MEAULTE, 9th Devons at BUIRE and XVth Corps Headquarter troops, 7th Divisional Artillery & 7th Div'l Train at HEILLY, and clean underclothing was issued. The section lorry conveyed clothing to the bath houses at MEAULTE and BUIRE and also to BOVES. A lorry from the Divisional Supply Column also carried clothing between HEILLY and BOVES. Paid the laundresses at BOVES for washing & repairing underclothing. Reported at the A.D.M.S's office at 6 p.m. F. S. Carson, Capt.	
BUIRE-sur-l'Ancre	18/8/16		General inspections of sanitary arrangements in the Divisional Area. Visited the laundry and bath-house at HEILLY and inspected part of the village of BUIRE. Reports received from the inspectors of the section shewing improvement	

WAR DIARY
or
INTELLIGENCE SUMMARY
(Erase heading not required.)

Army Form C. 2118.

Instructions regarding War Diaries and Intelligence Summaries are contained in F. S. Regs., Part II. and the Staff Manual respectively. Title Pages will be prepared in manuscript.

Place	Date	Hour	Summary of Events and Information	Remarks and references to Appendices
			of the sanitation of the area.	

No 20929 Pte H Cockran, 9th Devons was reported as a case of suspected Enteric. the case was investigated, the billet disinfected & the usual instructions given re-contacts.

Instructions have been received of the area allotted by the XV th Corps to the 7th Division for sanitary supervision.

N.C.O's and men of the 20th Manchesters & 2nd R Warwicks were bathed at BUIRE, the 1st South Staffords at MEAULTE and XV th Corps troops, 23rd Field Ambulance & 7th Division Artillery at HEILLY.

The Section lorry carried clothing between HEILLY and MEAULTE bath house

Lieut E B Barnes RAMC who was attached to the Sanitary Section for instruction in the method of sanitation to be carried out, was instructed to report back to the 21st Field Ambulance -

I reported at the A D M S's office at 6 p.m.

F. S. Carson. Capt.

2449 Wt. W14957/M90 750,000 1/16 J.B.C. & A. Forms/C.2118/12.

WAR DIARY or INTELLIGENCE SUMMARY

Army Form C. 2118.

(Erase heading not required.)

Place	Date	Hour	Summary of Events and Information	Remarks and references to Appendices
BUIRE sur-l-Ancre	19/8/16		The Section is continuing the Sanitation duties in the various areas. I inspected the 91st Brigade area. I again inspected DERNANCOURT village in the morning with Brig. General Steele, the Town Major of DERNANCOURT and the Medical Officers of the 22nd Brigade. The General commented on the amount of improvement in Sanitation that had been made. In the afternoon I met the Town Major of DERNANCOURT and the Medical Officers of the 22nd Infantry Brigade and made out a scheme of public latrines on the deep trench fly-proof system & other sanitary details. An N.C.O. of the Sanitary Section made a plan of DERNANCOURT shewing the sites of the various sanitary arrangements, for the Town Major's office. N.C.Os & men of the 2nd Royal Irish Regt and 22nd Brigade Machine Gun Coy were bathed at MEAULTE, 2nd Border Regt & 23rd Field Ambulance at BUIRE and XVth Corps troops, 23rd Field Ambulance & 7th Division Artillery at HEILLY. The section lorry carried clothing from HEILLY to the bath houses at BUIRE & MEAULTE. Laundresses at HEILLY were paid for washing & repairing clothing. I reported at the A.D.M.S's office at 6 p.m. F. S. Cowan Capt.	

WAR DIARY
or
INTELLIGENCE SUMMARY
(Erase heading not required.)

Army Form C. 2118.

Instructions regarding War Diaries and Intelligence Summaries are contained in F. S. Regs., Part II. and the Staff Manual respectively. Title Pages will be prepared in manuscript.

Place	Date	Hour	Summary of Events and Information	Remarks and references to Appendices
BUIRE Sur-l-Ancre	20/8/16		Inspectors & men of the Section are continuing the work in the areas alloted to them –	
			I inspected part of the village of RIBEMONT with Lieut Col Roch, D.A.D.M.S. 7th Division; and the Town Major, and made arrangements for further sanitary work to be carried out in the village –	
			No. 15793 Pte G. R. Counter, 8th Devons, was reported as a case of Cerebro-Spinal Meningitis. the Billet was disinfected and the usual instruction given re-contacts the A.D.M.S. was asked to arrange for the swabbing of the throats of the contacts for a possible "carrier" –	
			Lieut Mackenzie R.A.M.C. of the 21st Field Ambulance reported to the Sanitary Section for a short course of instruction in "Military Sanitation in the field"	
			N. C. Os & men of the 91st Brigade Headquarters, Grenade Coy, Trench Mortar Battery & Machine Gun Coy and the 22nd Brigade Trench Mortar Battery were bathed at MEAULTE, the 20th Brigade Hdqrs, Trench Mortar Battery & Machine Gun Coy the 22nd Brigade Grenade Coy and 23rd Field Ambulance at BUIRE, the XV Corps Hdqr troops & 24th Manchesters at HEILLY and clean clothing was issued the Section lorry conveyed clothing between HEILLY and BOVES.	
			F. S. Carson, Capt.	

WAR DIARY
or
INTELLIGENCE SUMMARY

(Erase heading not required.)

Army Form C. 2118.

Instructions regarding War Diaries and Intelligence Summaries are contained in F. S. Regs., Part II. and the Staff Manual respectively. Title Pages will be prepared in manuscript.

Place	Date	Hour	Summary of Events and Information	Remarks and references to Appendices
BUIRE sur-l-Ancre	21/3/16		The Inspectors from the Sanitary Section have been in H.Q. areas & reported on the sanitation. With the D.a.D.M.S., I completed the inspection of RIBEMONT. At the request of the T.O. Officer, 2nd R. Irish Regt. an N.C.O. from the Sanitary Section was temporarily attached to that unit to instruct the Sanitary personnel in Sanitary arrangements. A man from the Sanitary Section was detailed to test water at the various water supplies in the Divisional area & put up notices indicating the amount of bleaching powder required. Notice boards for this are being made & printed by the Section. N.C.O's and men of the 22nd Manchesters were bathed at RIBEMONT, the 2nd Gordons at BUIRE, XVth Corps Hdqr. troops, 7th Divisional Train & 7th Divisional Artillery at HEILLY, and clean under clothing was issued. The Section lorry carried clothing between HEILLY and BUIRE. S. Caven Capt.	

WAR DIARY
or
INTELLIGENCE SUMMARY
(Erase heading not required.)

Instructions regarding War Diaries and Intelligence Summaries are contained in F. S. Regs., Part II. and the Staff Manual respectively. Title Pages will be prepared in manuscript.

Army Form C. 2118.

Place	Date	Hour	Summary of Events and Information	Remarks and references to Appendices
BUIRE Sur-l-Ancre	22/3/16		Men of the Section engaged in Routine sanitary work in the various areas	

I inspected & reported upon the area at HEILLY vacated by the 4th Brigade R.H.A, 35th & 87th Batteries R.F.A. and Divisional Ammunition Column with the D.A.D.M.S — Lt Col Rock —

Enlarged map shewing Brigade areas made & sent to the A.D.M.S's office

Making & printing notice boards to shew amount of bleaching powder required for the various water supplies in the area —

N.C.Os & men of the 22nd Manchesters were bathed at MEAULTE, 24th Manchesters, 1st R Welsh Fusiliers & 22nd Field Ambulance at BUIRE and XVth Corps Headquarter troops & 7th Divisional Train at HEILLY, clean clothing was issued —

No 451 Pte E Rainford of the 1st London Sanitary Coy R.A.M.C. T reported as a reinforcement from No 1 Territorial Base Depot, Rouen —

The Section lorry carried clothing between HEILLY and BOVES.

Reported at the A.D.M.S's office at 6 p m —

F. S. Cavan, Capt.

WAR DIARY
or
INTELLIGENCE SUMMARY

(Erase heading not required.)

Army Form C. 2118.

Place	Date	Hour	Summary of Events and Information	Remarks and references to Appendices
BUIRE Sur l'Ancre	23/8/16		The inspectors of the Sanitary Section continue their general routine work in their areas.	

I inspected the 91st Company R.E.'s at E Hd (Albert combined sheet). their lines were found very insanitary and a written report was sent to the A.D.M.S.

A case of suspected Dysentery was reported in the 109th Railway Co R.E. supposed to be stationed at BUIRE; the Company had moved and the telegram notifying the A.D.M.S. has been returned. No 1433 Pte Mellor of the 24th Manchesters was reported as a case of Paratyphoid "B"; the case has been investigated & the usual instructions given.

N.C.O.'s & men of the 8th Devons were bathed at BUIRE, 20th Manchesters at MEAULTE and XV Corps Troops & 7th Divisional Train at HEILLY, clean clothing was issued.

The Section lorry carried clothing between HEILLY and the bath houses at BUIRE and MEAULTE.

The men of the section & attached men were paid.

I reported at the A.D.M.S.'s office at 6 p.m.

F. S. Carsen, Capt.

WAR DIARY
or
INTELLIGENCE SUMMARY

(*Erase heading not required.*)

Army Form C. 2118.

Instructions regarding War Diaries and Intelligence Summaries are contained in F. S. Regs., Part II. and the Staff Manual respectively. Title Pages will be prepared in manuscript.

Place	Date	Hour	Summary of Events and Information	Remarks and references to Appendices
BUIRE sur-l-Ancre	24/8/16		Men of the Section carried on the routine work in the Divisional area. I inspected the bath-houses and laundry at HEILLY. The civilians employed in laundry work at BOVES have been paid. N.C.O's and men of the 2nd Queens & 20th Manchesters were bathed at MEAULTE, 9th Devons at BUIRE and XV th Corps troops & 7th Divisional Train at HEILLY, clean clothing was issued. The Section lorry carried clothing between HEILLY and the bath-houses at BUIRE and MEAULTE. A lorry from the supply column carried clothing between HEILLY and BOVES. I reported at the A.D.M.S.'s office at 6 p.m. F. S. Carson Capt.	
BUIRE sur-l-Ancre area	25/8/16		General routine work was carried out in the sub-areas. The reports of the inspectors show a great improvement in the sanitation & prevalence (reduction of) of flies in the areas occupied by the various units in the Divisional area. Deep trench fly-proof public latrines are completed in the whole area & all the sanitary arrangements are now completed.	

2449 Wt. W14957/M90 750,000 1/16 J.B.C. & A. Forms/C.2118/12.

WAR DIARY or INTELLIGENCE SUMMARY

(Erase heading not required.)

Army Form C. 2118.

Instructions regarding War Diaries and Intelligence Summaries are contained in F. S. Regs., Part II. and the Staff Manual respectively. Title Pages will be prepared in manuscript.

Place	Date	Hour	Summary of Events and Information	Remarks and references to Appendices
			I visited the bath houses at BUIRE and MEAULTE & paid the men of the 23rd Field Ambulance working there. Reports have been received from several inspectors that the sanitation of troops in the Divisional area but not belonging to the 7th Division is bad — open deep & shallow trench latrines are in use — horse manure is scattered over the areas occupied & flies are numerous. This applies particularly to the area west of DERNANCOURT. I inspected the portion of this area occupied by the horse lines of the 33rd Division R.F.A. and found that the lines were dirty, open latrines & billet refuse thrown onto manure heaps, there was no incinerator and flies were numerous. This was reported to the A.D.M.S. NCO's & men of the 2nd R. Irish Regt & 1st R. Welsh Fusiliers were bathed at BUIRE, the 1st South Staffords, 95th Field Co. R.E. & 21st Manchesters at MEAULTE and the XV Corps troops, 8th Devons, 7th Divisional Train & 23rd Field Ambulance at HEILLY; clean clothing was issued. The Section lorry carried clothing between HEILLY and MEAULTE and BUIRE. I reported at the A.D.M.S's office at 6 p.m.	F. S. Carson Capt.

WAR DIARY
or
INTELLIGENCE SUMMARY

(Erase heading not required.)

Army Form C. 2118.

Instructions regarding War Diaries and Intelligence Summaries are contained in F. S. Regs., Part II. and the Staff Manual respectively. Title Pages will be prepared in manuscript.

Place	Date	Hour	Summary of Events and Information	Remarks and references to Appendices
BUIRE sur-l-Ancre	26/9/16		General routine work in sanitation was carried on throughout the area. The water carts of the 91st Brigade have been inspected & the sources of supply visited. I rode to CORBIE to see the Officer in charge of the Advanced Medical Stores re-Arsenite of Soda for fly destruction. The 22nd Infantry Brigade have vacated DERNANCOURT, the area has been left in a very satisfactory condition. The laundresses at HEILLY were paid for their week's work. I inspected the manure dumps in the BUIRE area. N.C.O's & men of the 2nd Border Regt were bathed at BUIRE, the 20th Manchesters at MEAULTE, and the XV th Corps troops & 20th Battalion County of London Regiment at HEILLY – clean clothing was issued to 7th Div. troops. The Section lorry carried clothing between HEILLY and the bath-houses at BUIRE and MEAULTE. A lorry from the Divisional Supply Column was engaged in conveying clothing between HEILLY and BOVES. I reported at the A.D.M.S's office at 6 p.m. F. S. Carson Capt.	

2449 Wt. W14957/M90 750,000 1/16 J.B.C. & A. Forms/C.2118/12.

Place	Date	Hour	Summary of Events and Information	Remarks and references to Appendices
BUIRE sur-l-Ancre	27/8/16		General routine work. The N.C.O. & men of the Section were withdrawn from DERNANCOURT and the men sent to RIBEMONT. The several sources of water supply at BUIRE were tested & were labelled accordingly. NCO's & men of the 91st Brigade Trench Mortar Battery, Grenade Coy and Machine Gun Coy and also the 2nd Queens Regt were bathed at MEAULTE, the 20th Brigade Machine Gun Coy & Trench Mortar Battery at BUIRE and the XVth Corps troops and 20th Battalion County of London Regt at HEILLY. Clean clothing was issued to 7th Division troops. The Section lorry conveyed clothing between HEILLY and BOVES. I reported to the ADMS office at 6pm. F.S. Craven Capt.	

WAR DIARY
or
INTELLIGENCE SUMMARY

(Erase heading not required.)

Army Form C. 2118.

Instructions regarding War Diaries and Intelligence
Summaries are contained in F. S. Regs., Part II.
and the Staff Manual respectively. Title Pages
will be prepared in manuscript.

Place	Date	Hour	Summary of Events and Information	Remarks and references to Appendices
BUIRE sur-l-Ancre	28/9/16		Routine inspections & sanitation was carried on throughout the area. The area vacated by the 91st Infantry Brigade was inspected & found to have been left in a clean & sanitary condition. The 20th Brigade water carts were examined & the sources of supply visited — several chlorine tests were made & notice boards fixed. No 18883 Pte Wheeldon, 2nd Border Regt and No 27153 Pte Partington 2nd R Warwicks Regt were reported as suffering from Dysentery; the usual investigations were made & instructions given re-contacts; the bivouac occupied by Pte Partington was disinfected, the bivouac of Pte Wheeldon had been removed and the position could not be located. Under instructions from the D.D.M.S XVth Corps the horse drawn Thresh disinfector was sent from HEILLY to the XVth Corps Casualty Clearing Station near DERNANCOURT: a man of the Sanitary Section was sent to give instructions in the working of the machine. 2/Cpl W.J. Mills, No 2018, of the Sanitary Section was sent to the 23rd Field Ambulance suffering from acute Diarrhoea. N.C.O's & men of the 2nd Gordon Highlanders were bathed at BUIRE, 21st Manchesters at MEAULTE and XVth Corps troops, 7th Divisional train,	

2449 Wt. W14957/M90 750,000 1/16 J.B.C. & A. Forms/C.2118/12.

WAR DIARY
or
INTELLIGENCE SUMMARY

Army Form C. 2118.

Instructions regarding War Diaries and Intelligence Summaries are contained in F. S. Regs., Part II. and the Staff Manual respectively. Title Pages will be prepared in manuscript.

(Erase heading not required.)

Place	Date	Hour	Summary of Events and Information	Remarks and references to Appendices
BUIRE sur Ancre	29/3/16		12th Sherwood Forresters & 47th Division Trench Mortar Battery at HEILLY. Clean clothing was issued to 7th Division troops. The Section lorry carried clothing from HEILLY to the bath houses at BUIRE and MEAULTE and to BOVES. F. S. Carson. Capt. General inspections & sanitation was carried on in the Divisional area. The area occupied by the 24th Division units near DERNANCOURT rail head, was inspected & suggestions made in regard to sanitation. The billets occupied by the 7th Divisional Headquarters at FRICOURT were sprayed with disinfectant. An N.C.O. & man of the Sanitary Section were sent to the clothes store at HEILLY to take a detailed stock of the clothing there. The men attached to the bath house at HEILLY were paid. N.C.O's and men of the 22nd Manchesters were bathed at MEAULTE and XVth Corps troops, 7th Divisional Train & 12th Sherwood Forresters at HEILLY. Clean clothing was issued to 7th Division troops. The Section lorry carried clothing between the bath houses at BUIRE & MEAULTE from HEILLY and a Divisional lorry was sent to BOVES. I reported at the A.D.M.S's office at 6pm. F. S. Carson Capt	

WAR DIARY
or
INTELLIGENCE SUMMARY

(Erase heading not required.)

Army Form C. 2118.

Instructions regarding War Diaries and Intelligence Summaries are contained in F. S. Regs., Part II. and the Staff Manual respectively. Title Pages will be prepared in manuscript.

Place	Date	Hour	Summary of Events and Information	Remarks and references to Appendices
BUIRE sur-l.Ancre	30/8/16		The Inspectors of the Sanitary Section continued their inspections in the areas allotted to them	

The Inspectors of the Sanitary Section continued their inspections in the areas allotted to them

I visited FRICOURT and inspected the sanitary arrangements

An N.C.O. of the Sanitary Section was sent to supervise the sanitary arrangements of the Divisional Headquarters at FRICOURT.

An NCO and man of the Section were sent to MAMETZ to inspect the areas occupied by 7th Division troops.

The stock taking of clothing at HEILLY was completed

The man sent to the XVth Corps Casualty Clearing Station near DERNANCOURT with the horse drawn Thresh disinfector returned to HEILLY.

N.C.O's and men of the 8th Devons were bathed at BUIRE, 1st R.Welsh Fusileers at MEAULTE and XVth Corps troops at HEILLY - clean clothing was issued.

The section lorry carried clothing between HEILLY and the bath houses at BUIRE and MEAULTE

I reported at the A.D.M.S.'s office at 6 p.m.

F. S. Carson. Capt.

2449 Wt. W14957/M90 750,000 1/16 J.B.C. & A. Forms/C.2118/12.

WAR DIARY
or
INTELLIGENCE SUMMARY

(Erase heading not required.)

Army Form C. 2118.

Place	Date	Hour	Summary of Events and Information	Remarks and references to Appendices
BUIRE sur-l-Ancre	31/8/16		General inspections were made in the Divisional area. Monthly accounts were prepared and sent to the Base Paymaster. Inspections were continued in FRICOURT and MAMETZ. Two "P.B." men attached to the Sanitary Section were sent to FRICOURT to provide sanitary conveniences for Divisional Headquarters. N.C.O's and men of the 9th Devons were bathed at BUIRE, 1st Royal Welsh Fusiliers & 20th Manchesters at MEAULTE and XVth Corps troops & 7th Divisional Train at HEILLY — clean clothing was issued. The Section lorry carried clothing between HEILLY and the bath houses at MEAULTE, and a Divisional lorry carried clothing between HEILLY and BOVES. I reported at the A.D.M.S's office at 6pm. F. S. Carver. Capt.	

VII Divn. Sanitary Arrangements

Disposal of Urine

Urine Pit

Scale 1 ft / 24

SECTION
- Wooden Cover
- Superimposed Creosol drums
- Impervious Paving
- Turves
- Soil
- Burnt Tins, Soil, Cinders and Rubble
- Pit

PLAN
- Edge of Soil
- Paving
- Perforated Base
- 3'-0"

Kitchens

- Wooden fillet
- 3'-0"
- Sacking or Sandbag Boot or Bacon Box. 18"
- Bench
- Horseshoe weight
- Frame
- Movable shelf
- Leather hinges
- Ordinary Ration Box
- Portion of Biscuit Tin Perforated

Grease Pit

SECTION
- Hay
- Brick
- Paving
- Turves
- Soil
- This Soil etc.

PLAN
- Edge of Soil
- Cover
- Biscuit Tin
- Pit 3'-0"

Page 1

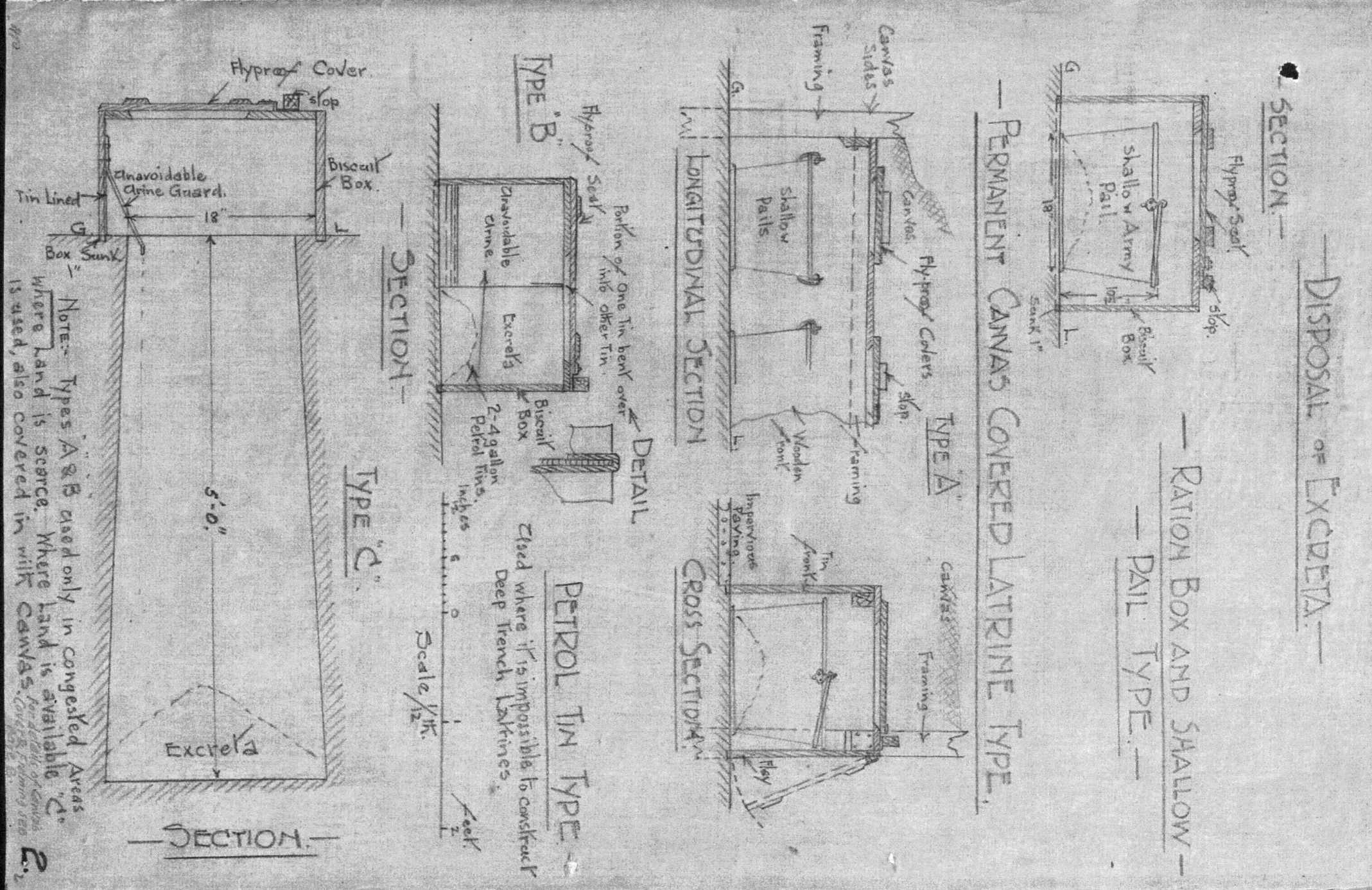

DISPOSAL OF EXCRETA Contd.

TYPE "C" C.P.

ELEVATION

- Lid Open
- Stop
- Tin Lined Biscuit Box
- Box sunk 1"
- G.L.
- Biscuit Tin for Paper
- Lid shut.
- Turves
- Brushwood & Soil
- Impervious Paving

Scale 1/2" = 1 ft

PLAN

- Biscuit Box
- Earth Edge
- slope
- Grass
- Lid Closed
- Turves
- Edge of Trench
- Impervious Paving

ISOMETRIC PROJECTION

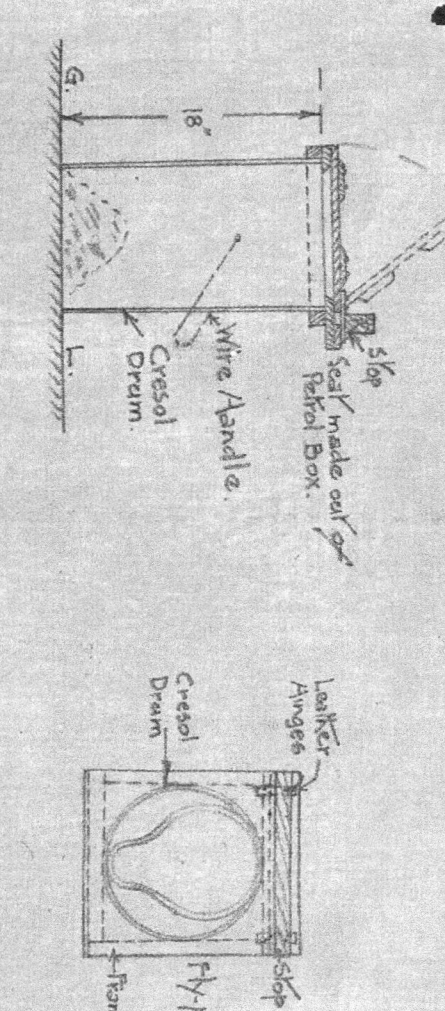
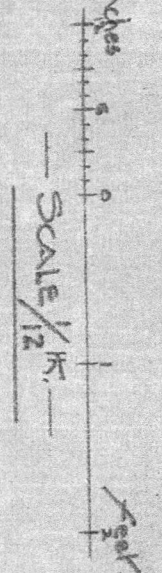
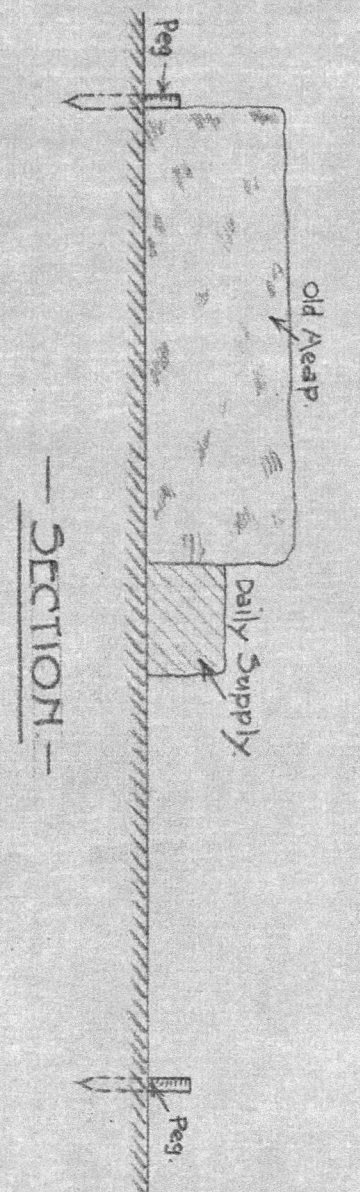
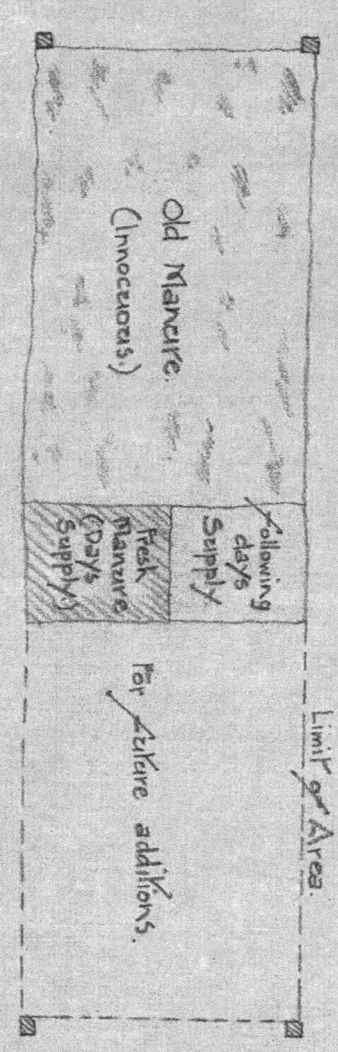

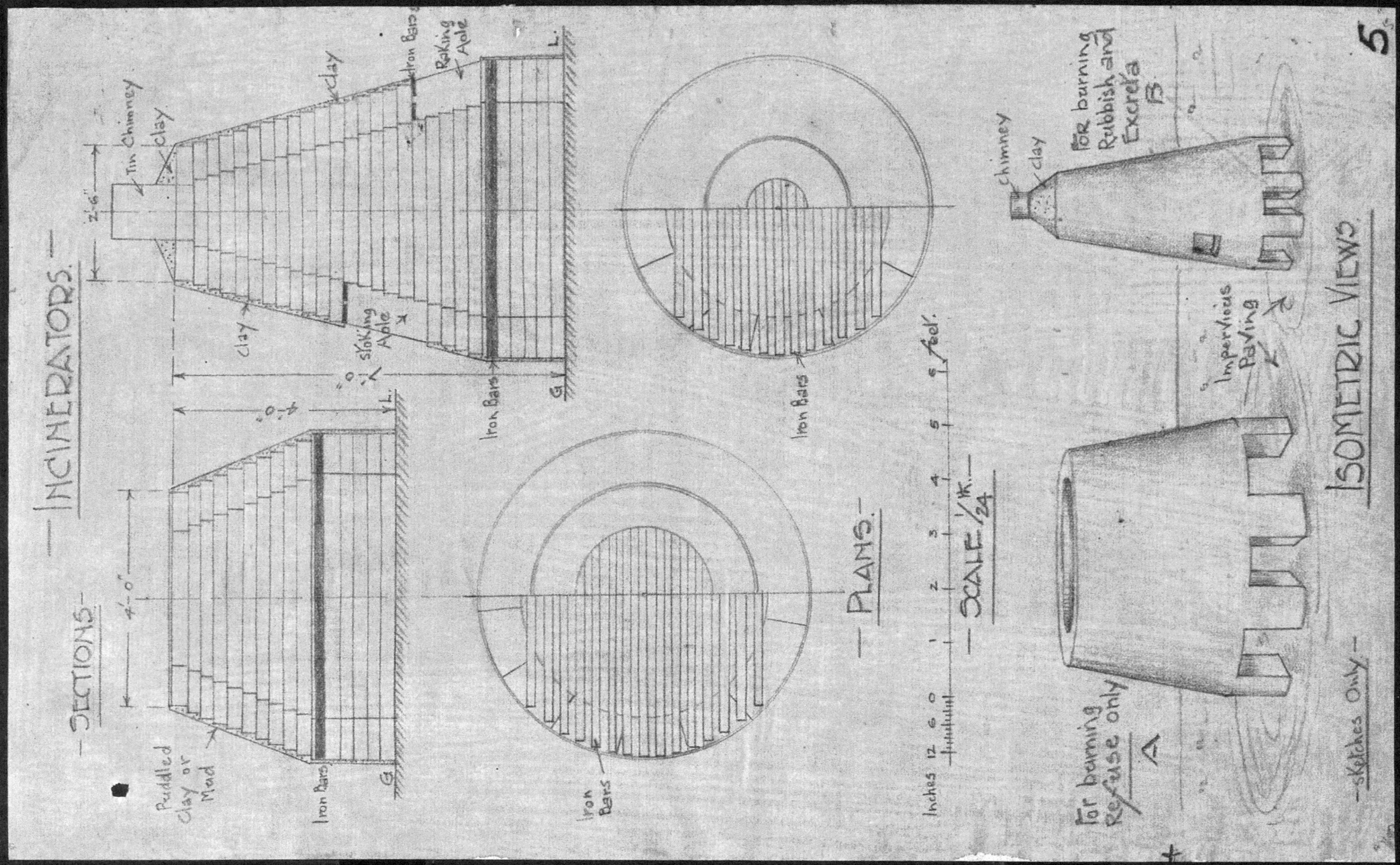

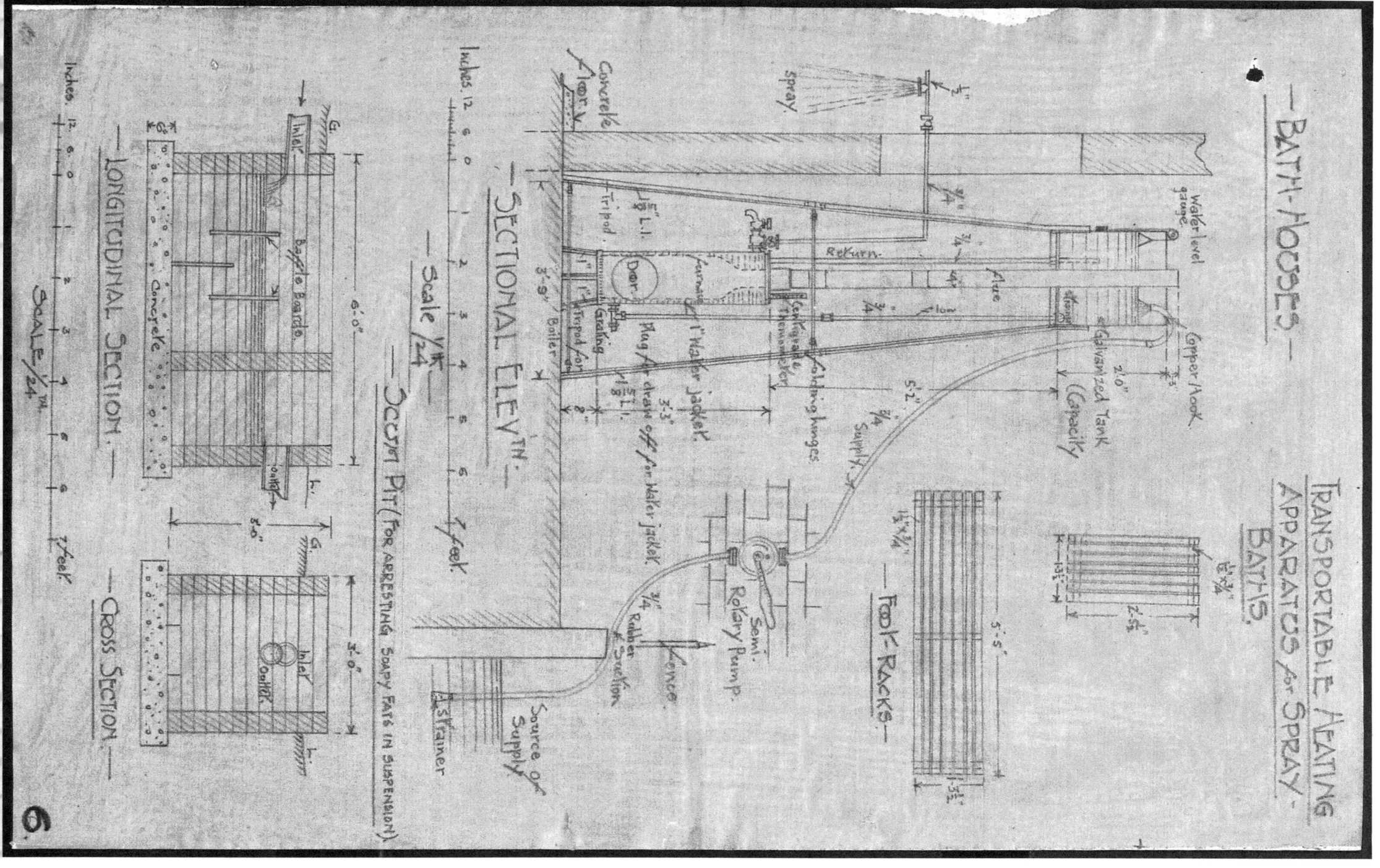

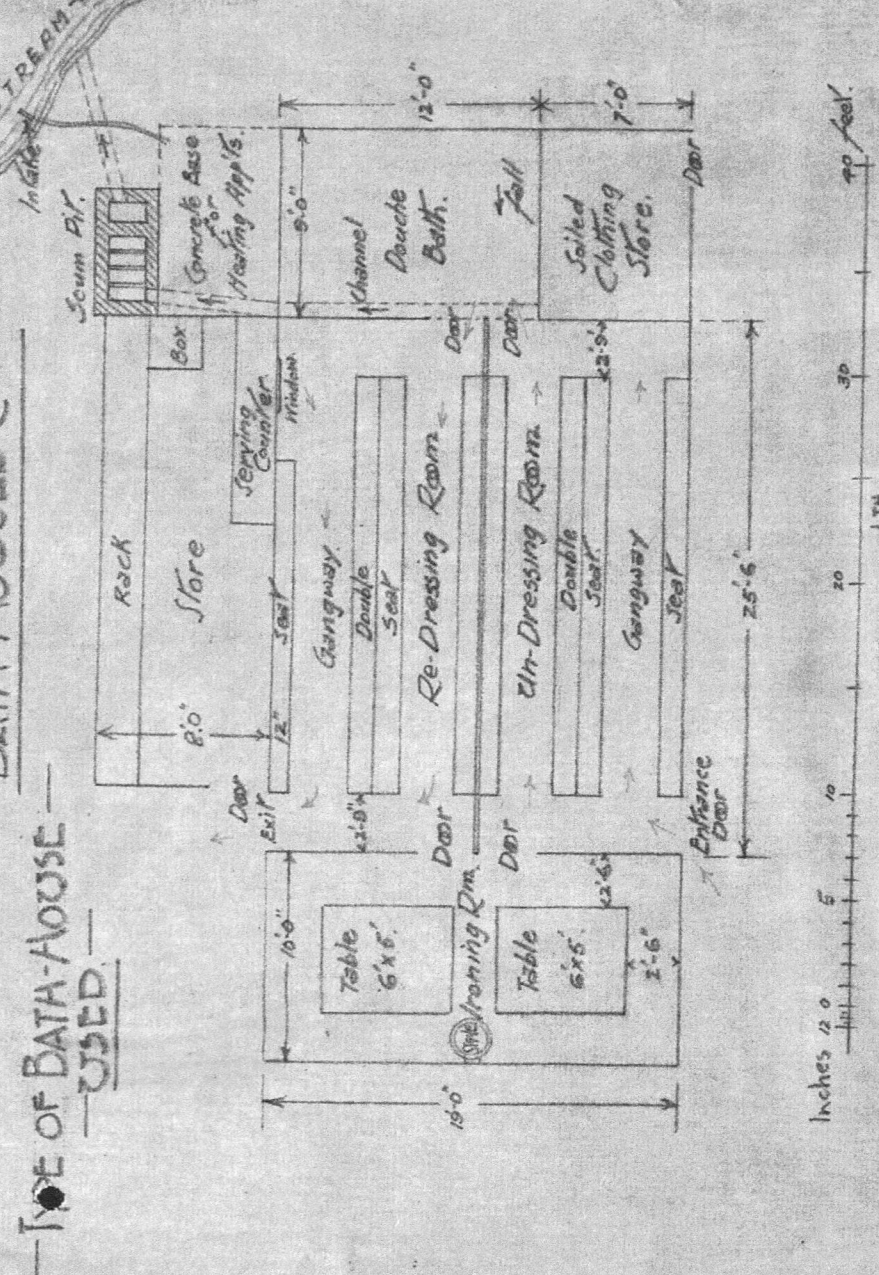
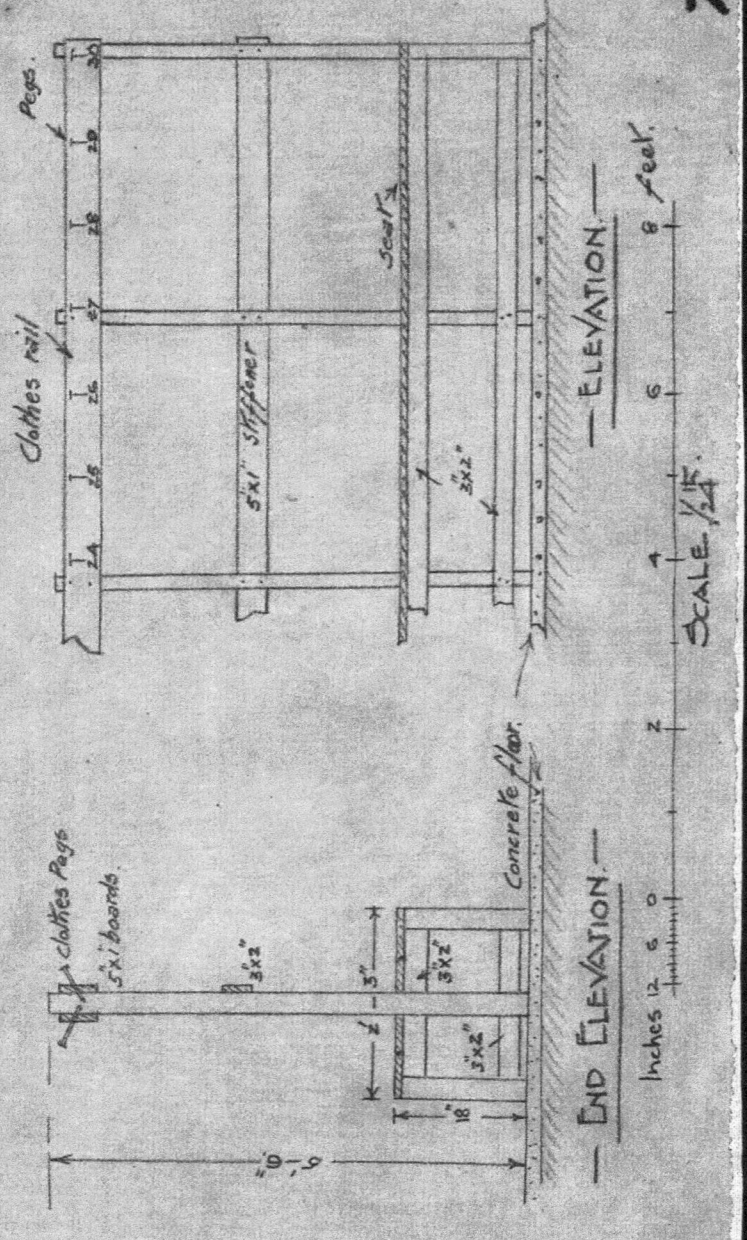

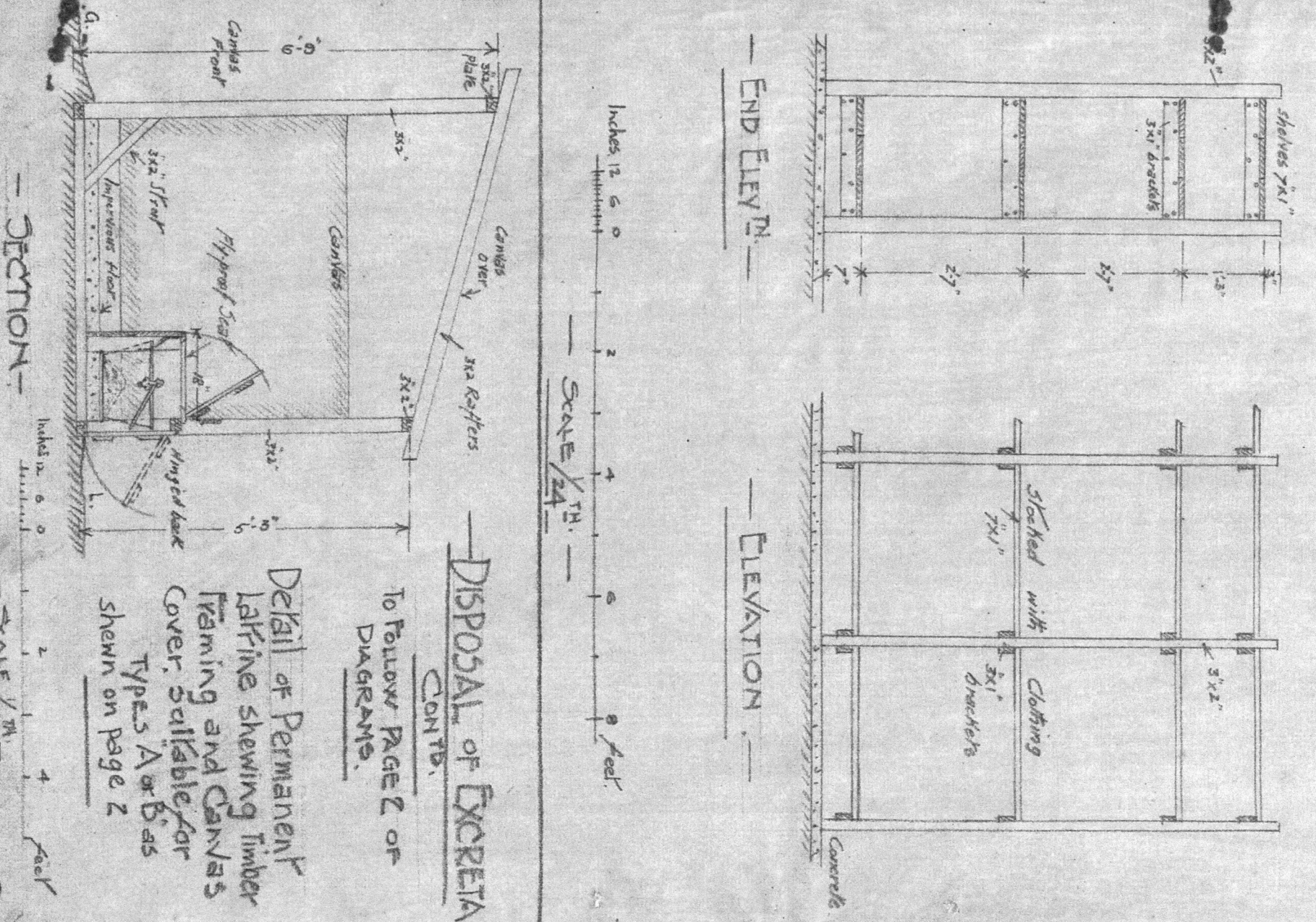

140/1188

CONFIDENTIAL

Section 10 —
2nd London Sanitary Cy RAMC, T.

attached to
7th Division —
B. E. Force - FRANCE -

Vol II

10th Sanitary Section

War Diary —

— Vol 2. —

from 1st September 1916 to 30th September 1916

Sept 1916.

COMMITTEE FOR THE
MEDICAL HISTORY OF THE WAR

Date   -2 DEC. 1916

WAR DIARY or INTELLIGENCE SUMMARY

(Erase heading not required.)

Army Form C. 2118.

Place	Date	Hour	Summary of Events and Information	Remarks and references to Appendices
BUIRE sur-l-Ancre	1/9/16		Routine inspections of the Divisional area were continued. The N.C.Os & men stationed at FRICOURT and MAMETZ continued the inspection of the sanitation carried out in that area. The monthly statements of accounts were prepared & sent to the Command Paymaster. The testing of water for amount of Chlorine to be added was continued. The case of Dysentery (Lieut Corbishley) in the 8th Devons was investigated and the billet disinfected. NCO's & men of the 20th Manchester, 2nd R Warwicks & 2nd R Irish Regt were bathed at MEAULTE and XV Corps troops at HEILLY – Clean clothing was issued. F. S. Carson Capt.	
BUIRE sur-l-Ancre	2/9/16		The area near DERNACOURT recently occupied by the 43rd & 44th Field Ambulance was inspected & found to have been left in a dirty state. The matter was reported to the A.D.M.S. The unsatisfactory condition of the Camps for German prisoners at EDGE HILL and MEAULTE was reported to the A.D.M.S.	

WAR DIARY
or
INTELLIGENCE SUMMARY.

(Erase heading not required.)

Army Form C. 2118.

Hour, Date, Place	Summary of Events and Information	Remarks and references to Appendices
BUIRE-sur-l'Ancre 3.9.16	Routine inspections were carried out by the Inspectors of the Division and the sanitation of RIBEMONT, BUIRE, MAMETZ and FRICOURT were improved. Supplies of water from the well at MONTAUBAN were obtained and the Bldarius was carried out. Garbage pits for village refuse were made at the MEAULTE rest camp. N.C.O's men of the 22nd Brigade Parade for Machine Gun key, Trench Mortar Battery & Headquarters were billeted at MEAULTE, and XV Corps troops at HEILLY - Been working on T.S. Carnoy are round. Routine inspections were continued & sanitation of the villages in the Divisional area improved. 80 men of RIBEMONT cleaning the billets & sanitary area commenced. were moved and given to the four snipers. Convoys of extra women for getting fires were made ready for issue & tests will soon be made. The use of Egineries (W/5293 General) in forward lights	

WAR DIARY or INTELLIGENCE SUMMARY.

Army Form C. 2118.

(Erase heading not required.)

Hour, Date, Place	Summary of Events and Information	Remarks and references to Appendices
	attached to "A" Coy, 9th Devons was investigated and disinfection carried out. N.C.O.'s and men of the 20th Bgde Headquarters, Machine Gun Coy & Trench Mortar Battery were bathed at BUIRE. Clean clothing was issued. I reported at the A.D.M.S office at 6 p.m. F. S. Carson. Capt.	
BUIRE-sur-l-Ancre 4/9/16	Routine inspections of the area were continued & the sanitation of the villages in the Divisional area supervised by the men of the Section. Two attached men were brought from HEILLY and RIBEMONT to attend to the sanitation of BUIRE-sur-l-Ancre The two men of the section who were stationed at MAMETZ were withdrawn. Enquiries were made re the cases of Dysentery - No. 17211 Pte Williams, 1st R. Welsh Fus, No. 9799A Pte Barnard, 22nd Bgde R.F.A, No 10254 Pte Fitzgerald 14th Bgde R.A.D. The billets of the 20th Brigade units, vacated yesterday, were inspected & rubbish that had been left was burnt. N.C.O's & men of XV Corps troops, 7th Divnl train and New Zealand Field Ambulance were bathed at HEILLY. I reported at the A.D.M.S. office at 6 p.m.	

WAR DIARY
or
INTELLIGENCE SUMMARY.

Army Form C. 2118.

Hour, Date, Place	Summary of Events and Information	Remarks and references to Appendices
BUIRE-sur-l-Ancre 5/9/16	Routine instructions & inspection of companies were continued. The men received by 1st Division Depot were inspected by men of the section & copies of the plan of RIBEMONT showing billets & sanitary areas, were given to the Town Mayor. I reported at the R.A.D's office at 6 p.m. NCO's men of the 2nd Gordon Highlanders were posted at MEAULTE and XV Corps Troops, 1st Gwent Town & New Zealand Field Ambulance at HEILLY — clean clothing was issued to the Gen Base Depot.	T.S. Gwen. Coll.
BUIRE-sur-l-Ancre 6/9/16	General instructions & continuation of the previous one were continued. I inspected the billet zones at BUIRE — one of the section & attached men were found. NCO's men of the 20th Bgde Machine Gun Coy, Grenade Coy, Trench Mortar Battery & Headquarters, also the 2nd	

WAR DIARY
or
INTELLIGENCE SUMMARY.

(Erase heading not required.)

Army Form C. 2118.

Instructions regarding War Diaries and Intelligence Summaries are contained in F. S. Regs., Part II. and the Staff Manual respectively. Title pages will be prepared in manuscript.

Hour, Date, Place	Summary of Events and Information	Remarks and references to Appendices
BUIRE-sur-l-ANCRE 7/9/16	Royal Warwicks & 1st Royal Welsh Fus, were bathed at BUIRE, 1st South Staffords at MEAULTE, XV Corps troops & 7th Div'nl train at HEILLY. Clean clothing was issued. I reported at the A.D.M.S's office at 6 p.m F.S. Cairn. Capt I accompanied Brig. General Steele on a visit of inspection of the billets occupied by the 22nd Infantry Brigade, in BUIRE Routine inspections & supervision of village sanitation were continued. The men of the Section and attached men were withdrawn from FRICOURT. The case of Diphtheria. No 5457 Pte Sartin of the 2/4th Glocesters, attached to 9th Devons was investigated and the billet disinfected. I reported to the A.D.M.S. upon the large amount of sirops mixed with unpurified water, that were sold	

Hour, Date, Place	Summary of Events and Information	Remarks and references to Appendices
BUIRE-sur-l-Ancre 8/9/16.	... in the Bivouac area & the probable effects or report to superiors. N.C.O's and men of 24th Manchesters were billeted at MEAULTE, 2nd R. Scots, 2nd R. Warwicks, 1st R. Welch and 20th Manchesters at BUIRE and XV Divn Bakery and 17th Bn London Regt at HEILLY. Clean clothing was issued to 1st Devon Regt. I reported at the S.O.M's office at 6 p.m. & went to Camp 04. I reported at the S.O.M's office at 9.30 a.m. and visited the late MEAULTE. Routine inspection of the Bivouaced area was continued & the area vacated by the 1st Devon Regt inspected. Disinfection of latrines in BUIRE and RIBEMONT was continued. The attached men at RIBEMONT returned to BUIRE. 1 N.C.O. in charge of the sanitation at Headquarters Bu...	

WAR DIARY or INTELLIGENCE SUMMARY.

Army Form C. 2118.

(*Erase heading not required.*)

Hour, Date, Place	Summary of Events and Information	Remarks and references to Appendices
	in FRICOURT was withdrawn. The men employed at the bath-houses at BUIRE and MEAULTE were paid. N.C.O's & men of 91st Brigade Machine Gun Co, Grenade Co & Trench Mortar Battery also 1st South Staffords and 2nd Queens were bathed at MEAULTE and XV Corps troops at HEILLY. Clean clothing was issued. F. S. Carson, Capt	
BUIRE-sur-l-Ancre 9/9/16	Samples of sirops as sold to the troops were taken by a Bacteriologist from XV Corps & tested — The tests proved that the drinks were unsatisfactory, at one house it was found to be very bad & the house was officially put "out of bounds". I visited the new area round AIRAINES with the D.A.D.M.S. with a view to finding out the type of sanitation required and sites were chosen for Brigade bath-houses at AIRAINES, HUPPY and FORCEVILLE and the bath-house for Divisional troops at HALLENCOURT.	

WAR DIARY
or
INTELLIGENCE SUMMARY.

(Erase heading not required.)

Army Form C. 2118.

Place	Hour, Date	Summary of Events and Information	Remarks and references to Appendices
BUIRE-sur-l-Ancre	6/9/16		

T.S. Counattack

Paraded at the Sports Ground at 9.30 a.m. and also invaded the back lanes at MEAULTE.

I travelled to AIRAINE 5 accompanied by train of the station on the return party which also conveyed equipment for a back lanes.

The lesson coincided our the BUIRE to join the 23rd Field Ambulance with the purpose of entraining for the new area.

The back lanes at MEAULTE were dismantled & equipment moved to HEILLY by the section lorry

Fatigue men were employed in cleaning up the billets at BUIRE vacated by the 22nd Brigade.

The fourteenance employed at HEILLY were four NCO's and men of the 22nd Manchesters men tested at MEAULTE and XV Corps Rest at HEILLY

Hour, Date, Place	Summary of Events and Information	Remarks and references to Appendices
AIRAINES 11/9/16	I visited FORCEVILLE with an N.C.O. & measured up site for proposed bath house & fixed billets for the section at HALLENCOURT. A scheme for the new bath house for FORCEVILLE was made and the estimate for material required sent to Divisional Headquarters. The Section & attached men marched from MEAULTE to the station at ALBERT where they entrained at 6 p.m with the 91st Infantry Brigade. The lorry attached to the Section was sent to the Divisional Supply Column workshop for repairs. Bathing & laundry work was continued at HEILLY. A bath fitting was fixed up at AIRAINES and seating arranged in the Dressing rooms. I reported at the A.D.M.S's office at 5.30 p.m. F. S. Carson Capt.	

Hour, Date, Place	Summary of Events and Information	Remarks and references to Appendices
AIRAINES 12/9/16	Arrangements were made for establishing half house at HUPPY and HALLENCOURT The section and attached men arrived at OISEMONT and detrained at 9 am. marched to HALLENCOURT & took over billets. The Ammunition area was divided & inspected. attended to the returns and area. I reported at the ADMS office at 9.30 am. t.s. Cannon Capt.	
HALLENCOURT 13/9/16	I visited the proposed half house at HUPPY and inspected the surrounding area. The Truck drawn draughter arrived at HALLENCOURT from HEILLY about 5 p.m. Three men of the 23rd Field Ambulance were sent with an N.C.O. of the section to take over the half house at HUPPY. The half house at HALLENCOURT was arranged	

WAR DIARY or INTELLIGENCE SUMMARY.

(Erase heading not required.)

Army Form C. 2118.

Hour, Date, Place	Summary of Events and Information	Remarks and references to Appendices
	and cleaned out ready for bathing. The following cases of Dysentery were investigated N° 20111 Pte Richards 22nd Manchesters & N° 9293 Pte Core 2nd Royal Irish Regt — the following case of Paratyphoid was also investigated N° 1537 Pte Stott, 2nd Gordon Hdrs. A "form of particulars" for N° 37626 Pte Pike the case of Dysentery in the 35th Brigade R.F.A, was sent to the Medical Officer of that unit. I reported at the ADMS office at 6 p.m. F.S. Carron Capt.	
HALLENCOURT 14/9/16	I visited the bath-houses at AIRAINES and HUPPY, inspected the area occupied by the 20th Infantry Brigade & investigated the case of Dysentery — N° 18939 Pte Lewis of the 21st Manchesters. Arrangements were made for a supply of water to be obtained from the Mill at HALLENCOURT for the bath house in that village. A plan for the proposed bath-house at FORCEVILLE was made.	

WAR DIARY
or
INTELLIGENCE SUMMARY.
(Erase heading not required.)

Army Form C. 2118.

Instructions regarding War Diaries and Intelligence Summaries are contained in F. S. Regs., Part II. and the Staff Manual respectively. Title pages will be prepared in manuscript.

Hour, Date, Place	Summary of Events and Information	Remarks and references to Appendices
	Two cases of Scarlet Fever amongst the Civil population at FONTAINE-sur-SOMME notified by the Fourth Army; were investigated & report sent to the DDMS.	
	Bricks for an incinerator to be built in HALLENCOURT were purchased	
	Routine inspections were carried out in the Divisional area by the inspectors of the Section.	
	The lorry attached to the section conveyed the bath equipment & men to HUPPY.	
	A disinfection station was arranged at HALLENCOURT	
	Four lorries, supplied by the Divisional Supply Column brought clothing from HEILLY to AIRAINES	
	Clean clothing was sent from AIRAINES to the bath house at HUPPY.	
	On instructions from the A.D.M.S. an N.C.O. of the section was sent to supervise the sanitation of the rest camp at AULT	
	Reports from the inspectors shew that the area occupied by the Division was found in good condition but practically no sanitary arrangements were found.	

F. S. Carson
Capt.

(73989) W4141—463. 400,000. 9/14. H.&J.Ltd. Forms/C. 2118/10.

WAR DIARY or INTELLIGENCE SUMMARY.

Army Form C. 2118.

Hour, Date, Place	Summary of Events and Information	Remarks and references to Appendices
HALLENCOURT 15/9/16	I visited the site of the new bath house at FORCEVILLE with the O.C. 54th Field Co. RE and I also visited the bath houses at AIRAINES and HUPPY. General inspections were continued in the Divl. area. Water supplies were tested to shew the amount of Chlorine to be added for purification of the water & notice boards were fixed. NCOs and men of the 2nd Border Regiment were bathed at AIRAINES and the 2nd Queens at HUPPY. Clean clothing was issued. The dirty clothing from the bath houses were disinfected. Seats were fitted in the bath house at HUPPY. Maps are being prepared of the Divisional area shewing Sanitary arrangements & structures made by the Division.	

F. S. Carson
Capt.

WAR DIARY
or
INTELLIGENCE SUMMARY.

Army Form C. 2118.

Hour, Date, Place	Summary of Events and Information	Remarks and references to Appendices
HAILENCOURT 16/10/16	The following cases of dysentery were investigated No 27367 Pte Scott, 8th Queens, No 4682 Pte Bodinier, 2nd Queens Regt and No 2993 Pte Jacques of the 2nd Dorsetshire. The temperature at HEILLY was found normal. Routine inspections were continued in the Divisional Area. Water testing was carried on at the various watering points. These horses were outfitted by the Quar Supply between and all clothing brought from the Divisional at BOVES and the Fumature yard. Three lorry loads of clothing were brought to AIRAINES from HEILLY. The first house at HAILENCOURT HAPPY and AIRAINES were dismantled & clothing placed at AIRAINES when it was being packed ready for removal. The disinfection of clothing was continued I reported at the DDMS office at 6 p.m. T. S. Carson Capt.	

WAR DIARY
or
INTELLIGENCE SUMMARY.
(Erase heading not required.)

Army Form C. 2118.

Instructions regarding War Diaries and Intelligence Summaries are contained in F.S. Regs., Part II. and the Staff Manual respectively. Title pages will be prepared in manuscript.

Hour, Date, Place	Summary of Events and Information	Remarks and references to Appendices
HALLENCOURT 17/9/16	Arrangements were made for the removal to the new area. Three lorry loads of clothing were taken from AIRAINES and left at ABBEYVILLE station in charge of an N.C.O. of the section. The clothing & equipment of the bath house at HALLENCOURT were conveyed to AIRAINES. The packing of clothing for removal was continued. 340 men of the 24th Manchesters were bathed. F. S. Carson. Capt.	
HALLENCOURT 18/9/16	5000 changes of clean clothing were left at AIRAINES in charge of an N.C.O of the section to be taken over by the incoming Division. The Section and attached men moved from HALLENCOURT at 10.15 a.m. & marched to ABBEYVILLE where they entrained at 6.30 p.m. after loading the clothing into trucks. F. S. Carson. Capt.	

WAR DIARY
or
INTELLIGENCE SUMMARY.

(Erase heading not required.)

Army Form C. 2118.

Hour, Date, Place	Summary of Events and Information	Remarks and references to Appendices
BAILLEUL 19/9/16	The Section arrived at the detraining point at BAILLEUL at 1.30 a.m., the clothing was unloaded, put into lorries & taken to FLETRE when storage room was found. The Section marched from BAILLEUL and arrived at FLETRE about 8 a.m. The O.C. 19th Divisional Sanitary Section called upon me and discussed "the methods of sanitation in the new area." I started at the C.O's office at 2.30 p.m. F. S. Carson Capt.	
FLETRE 20/10/16	An N.C.O. and men from the Section were sent to the new area to secure experiences & first impressions of the sanitary arrangements & water supplies. Three N.C.O's of the section were sent to obtain information re the working of the Bath-house and Laundry at PONT DE NIEPPE and the bath house at PAPOT. (B. to a sheet 36.)	

WAR DIARY
or
INTELLIGENCE SUMMARY.

(*Erase heading not required.*)

Army Form C. 2118.

Instructions regarding War Diaries and Intelligence Summaries are contained in F.S. Regs., Part II. and the Staff Manual respectively. Title pages will be prepared in manuscript.

Hour, Date, Place	Summary of Events and Information	Remarks and references to Appendices
FLETRE 21/9/16	The N.C.O. left in charge of the bath house and laundry at HEILLY reported at FLETRE with the 5 men who had assisted him. The N.C.O. of the Section who had supervised the sanitation of the area occupied by XV Corps troops also reported at FLETRE. The Foden lorry with steam disinfector and also the motor lorry with Section equipment arrived at FLETRE from HALLENCOURT at 7.15 p.m. F. S. Carson, Capt. I visited the new area accompanied by 2 N.C.O's of the section and was shewn the bath houses at PAPOT, the PIGGERIES and the bath-house & laundry at PONT-DE-NIEPPE and also the chief water supplies in the area, by the O.C. 19th Divisional Sanitary Section. I visited the ADMS & discussed the question of the men required for water patrols, bath-house work & sanitation with him & the 7th Division Headquarters. F. S. Carson Capt.	

Hour, Date, Place	Summary of Events and Information	Remarks and references to Appendices
PONT DE NEIPPE 22/9/16	The Section moved from FLETRE at 8.30 a.m., marched to PONT-DE-NEIPPE and took up billets. 16 of the 26 men called for were provided by the Base Depot and posted by an N.C.O. of the section for under patrols & sanitary work in the Divisional area. An N.C.O. of the section and 3 men were posted at the PLOEGSTEERT outlets and one man at the other main outlets in the area, viz:- B9a, B11a, B8, B26d & B10b, about 36. An N.C.O. of the section and 6 men from the 29th Field Ambulance were on to take over the first house at PAPOT (B.3.c. about 36). The first house stationed at PONT-DE-NEIPPE was taken over from the 19th Division. 4 men were posted there for duty under 2 N.C.Os of the section. The Circulars were moved from FLETRE and installed at the first house at PONT DE NEIPPE.	

WAR DIARY
or
INTELLIGENCE SUMMARY.
(*Erase heading not required.*)

Army Form C. 2118.

Instructions regarding War Diaries and Intelligence Summaries are contained in F.S. Regs., Part II. and the Staff Manual respectively. Title pages will be prepared in manuscript.

Hour, Date, Place	Summary of Events and Information	Remarks and references to Appendices
	The clothing at FLETRE was conveyed & stored at the laundry at PONT DE NEIPPE by 2 lorries supplied by No 50 Supply Column and the Section lorry. The section lorry also conveyed the section equipment from FLETRE to PONT DE NEIPPE. The following clothing was taken over from the 19th Division at PAPOT and PONT DE NEIPPE, 2350 shirts, 2637 drawers, 2308 pr socks — all dirty. Clean clothing was sent to the bath house at PAPOT. F. S. Carson, Capt	
PONT DE NEIPPE 23/9/16	The men of the Section were posted to duties in the new area (roughly U 13, 14, 19, 20, 21, 25, 26 & 27 — T. 18, 23 & 24 — 25 to 30 on sheet 28 — The Divisional area was divided into sections for inspection. Water was tested for the amount of chlorine required at several supplies. One N.C.O., at the request of the Brig General of the	

WAR DIARY
or
INTELLIGENCE SUMMARY
(Erase heading not required.)

Army Form C. 2118.

Instructions regarding War Diaries and Intelligence Summaries are contained in F. S. Regs., Part II. and the Staff Manual respectively. Title Pages will be prepared in manuscript.

Place	Date	Hour	Summary of Events and Information	Remarks and references to Appendices
			22nd Infantry Brigade was sent to PAPOT to build the closed type of brick incinerator.	

Investigation of the cases of suspected Dysentery – No 5/43515 Ptte W Buchanan 2nd Gordon Hdrs and No. 106897 Pte E Tolson R.A.M.C. (21st F. Amb) – were made with a view to finding a "carrier"

The villages in the area have been inspected with a view to finding cases of infectious disease amongst civilians – no cases were found.

The civilians employed on sanitary work at NEIPPE and PONT-DE-NEIPPE were paid for their weeks work by arrangement with the O.C. 19th Divisional sanitary section.

Bath fittings were sent to "The Piggeries", (V. 19 c 1.9 sheet 28) in charge of an N.C.O. of the section, to be fitted up. Particulars of the material required for alterations to the building were sent to the A.D.M.S.

N.C.O's & men of 2nd Gordons, 21st Manchesters & 19th Dvn artillery were bathed at PONT-DE-NEIPPE, and 21st Manchesters & 91st Brigade M.G. Coy at PAPOT – clean clothing was issued.

Disinfection of clothing was carried out.

I reported at the A.D.M.S' office at 10 a.m.

2449 Wt. W14957/M90 750,000 1/16 J.B.C. & A. Forms/C.2118/12.

7. S. Carson Capt

WAR DIARY or INTELLIGENCE SUMMARY

Army Form C. 2118.

(Erase heading not required.)

Place	Date	Hour	Summary of Events and Information	Remarks and references to Appendices
PONT-DE-NEIPPE	24/9/16		Routine inspections were continued in the Divisional area. Men of the section and attached men were paid. Sanitation in NEIPPE and PONT-DE-NEIPPE was carried on. The cases of Dysentery — No 5292. 4th Gloucesters attached 9th Devons (Pte C. Page) and No 12188, Pte R. Pattison, 2nd Gordons — were investigated. Timber &c left by the 19th Divnl Sanitary Section was brought from PONT D'ACHELLE to PONT-DE-NEIPPE. Lieut Standing was attached to the Section for a short course of instruction in Military Hygiene before being posted to a unit. Reports for the inspectors of the section indicate that the area taken over by the Division is insanitary — Open pail latrines are found throughout the area. NCOs & men of 23rd Field Ambulance, 2nd Pontoon park & 19th Divnl artillery were bathed at PONT-DE-NEIPPE and 20th Manchesters at PAPOT. 1110 blankets of the 22nd Manchesters were disinfected. Women employed at the laundry did not work to-day. Pte McNaughton, A.S.C, M.T. attached to the section was sent, sick, to the 23rd Field Ambulance.	

F. S. Carson, Capt.

			WAR DIARY *or* INTELLIGENCE SUMMARY (*Erase heading not required.*)	Army Form C. 2118.

Instructions regarding War Diaries and Intelligence Summaries are contained in F. S. Regs., Part II. and the Staff Manual respectively. Title Pages will be prepared in manuscript.

Place	Date	Hour	Summary of Events and Information	Remarks and references to Appendices
PONT-DE NEIPPE	25/9/16		Routine inspections were continued throughout the area & supervision of scavenging & sanitation in NEIPPE and PONT-DE-NEIPPE was carried on.	
			The supervision of the water patrols was carried on & various water tests made for the amount of Chlorine required to be added.	
			The case of Dysentery, No 17275 Cpl F. Osborne, 1st R. Welsh Fusileers, was investigated with the view of finding a possible "carrier".	
			N.C.O's and men of the 24th Manchesters, 19th Divl Ammunition Column & Canadian A.S.C., were bathed at PONT-DE-NIEPPE, the 20th Manchesters, 2nd Warwicks, 22nd Bgde Machine Gun Cy, Grenade Cy, & Headquarters & also 21st Manchesters and 2nd R Irish Regt at PAPOT. Clean clothing was issued.	
			1115 blankets of the 2nd Border Regt were disinfected.	
			Laundry work was continued at PONT-DE-NEIPPE.	
			Pte S J Collinette No 2012 of this section was killed by an enemy shell fire in the grounds of the bath-house at PONT-DE-NEIPPE at 7 p.m.	

2449 Wt. W14957/M90 750,000 1/16 J.B.C. & A. Forms/C.2118/12.

7. S. Carson Capt.

WAR DIARY or INTELLIGENCE SUMMARY

(Erase heading not required.)

Army Form C. 2118.

Place	Date	Hour	Summary of Events and Information	Remarks and references to Appendices
PONT-DE-NEIPPE	26/9/16		Routine inspections were carried out in the area & also the scavenging & sanitation of NEIPPE and PONT-DE-NEIPPE. Water tests were made & notice boards fixed at the supply points. Tracing shewing the Divisional area was made, and also sketch plan shewing proposed alterations to the bath-house at PAPOT. N.C.O's and men of the 171st Coy R.E., 95th Coy R.E., 24th Manchesters & 19th Division Artillery were bathed at PONT-DE-NEIPPE; 7th Labour Battalion, 21st Manchesters, 2nd Warwicks, 2nd Queens, 91st Brigade signals, Divisional Signals, 91st Bgde M.G. Coy & 7th Divisional train at PAPOT. 1025 blankets of the 22nd Manchester Regt. were disinfected. Laundry work was continued at PONT-DE-NEIPPE. F.S. Carson Capt.	
PONT-DE-NEIPPE	27/9/16		Routine inspections were continued and the sanitation & scavenging of NEIPPE & PONT-DE-NEIPPE supervised. Water testing was continued. I had an interview with the C.O. 54th Field Coy R.E. about the proposed alterations to the bath-house at PAPOT.	

WAR DIARY
or
INTELLIGENCE SUMMARY

(Erase heading not required.)

Army Form C. 2118.

Instructions regarding War Diaries and Intelligence Summaries are contained in F. S. Regs., Part II. and the Staff Manual respectively. Title Pages will be prepared in manuscript.

Place	Date	Hour	Summary of Events and Information	Remarks and references to Appendices
			The case of Dysentery No 14816 Pte C Stoneman 9th Devons was investigated with a view of finding a possible "carrier".	
			Chart shewing cases of Dysentery which had occurred amongst the 7th Division troops was made & sent to the A.D.M.S.	
			N.C.O's and men of the 19th Division Artillery, 24th Manchesters & 9th Devons were bathed at PONT-DE-NEIPPE and 1st R Welsh Fusiliers at ⋯⋯T.	
			Laundry work was continued.	
			795 blankets of 9th Devons were disinfected.	
			4000 changes of underclothing (shirts, drawers & socks) were received from the Ordnance stores for the bath-houses.	
			Civilians employed at the laundry PONT-DE-NEIPPE were paid (this payment included about 1200 Francs for 19th Division work.	
			F. S. Carson. Capt	
PONT-DE -NEIPPE	28/9/16		Routine inspections & sanitation were carried on as yesterday.	
			I inspected the bath-house & laundry at PONT-DE-NEIPPE with the D.D.M.S. Capt Walshe.	
			Chlorine tests were applied to the water at various supply posts.	

2449 Wt. W14957/M90 750,000 1/16 J.B.C. & A. Forms/C.2118/12.

WAR DIARY or INTELLIGENCE SUMMARY

(Erase heading not required.)

Army Form C. 2118.

Place	Date	Hour	Summary of Events and Information	Remarks and references to Appendices
PONT-DE-NEIPPE	29/9/16		Public latrines were made at NEIPPE and at the bath house PONT-DE-NEIPPE. Incinerators are being built at NEIPPE and PAPOT by men attached to the Section. N.C.O's and men of the 171st Coy R.E's, 22nd Manchesters, 9th Devons, 7th Labour Battalion and 19th Division Artillery were bathed at PONT-DE-NEIPPE, 1st R. Welsh Fusileers & 22nd Manchesters at PAPOT and 2nd Queens Regt. at the PIGGERIES. Laundry work & disinfection of underclothing was carried on. F. S. Carson, Capt. I inspected the 9th Devons billeting area accompanied by Lieut Standing and S/Staff Sergt Williams. Routine inspections of the area and the sanitation of NEIPPE and PONT-DE-NEIPPE were continued. Public latrines are being built at NEIPPE. Brick incinerators are being built at PAPOT and PONT-DE-NEIPPE. I visited the water supply posts in the Divisional area. Chlorine tests were made & notice boards fixed at several supply posts	

WAR DIARY
or
INTELLIGENCE SUMMARY
(Erase heading not required.)

Army Form C. 2118.

Instructions regarding War Diaries and Intelligence Summaries are contained in F. S. Regs., Part II. and the Staff Manual respectively. Title Pages will be prepared in manuscript.

Place	Date	Hour	Summary of Events and Information	Remarks and references to Appendices
			Several notice boards for water chlorination were printed -	
			Box respirators for the section & attached men were obtained from the Divisional Gas school.	
			Civilians engaged in sanitary work were paid -	
			Lieut Standing returned to the 23rd Field Ambulance.	
			N.C.O's & men of the 9th Devons and 19th Division Artillery were bathed at PONT-DE-NEIPPE and, 1st R. Welsh Fusiliers & 22nd Brigade Grenade C.Y at PAPOT.	
			Underclothing from the bath-houses and 450 blankets from the 24th Manchesters were disinfected.	
			Laundry work was continued -	
			F. S. Carson. Capt	
PONT-DE-NEIPPE	30/9/16		Routine inspections in the area and sanitation in NEIPPE and PONT DE-NEIPPE were continued - and also the building of latrines and incinerators -	
			I inspected the billeting area occupied by the 2nd Queens Regt.	
			The case of Dysentery, No 32026, Pte Boulton, of the 21st Manchesters, was investigated with a view of finding a possible "carrier".	

WAR DIARY
or
INTELLIGENCE SUMMARY
(Erase heading not required.)

Army Form C. 2118.

Place	Date	Hour	Summary of Events and Information	Remarks and references to Appendices
			Water tests were made & the various sources of supply inspected. Notice boards were made & fixed to several supply posts. Monthly accounts were sent to Divisional Headquarters for approval. NCO's and men of the 9th Entrenching Battalion were bathed at PONT-DE-NIEPPE, 22nd Manchesters, 91st Bgde Machine Gun Coy and 7th Labour Battalion at PAPOT and 2nd Queens, 91st Bgde Grenade Coy & Trench Mortar Battery and the 86th Trench Mortar Battery at "The PIGGERIES". Laundry work was continued & underclothing disinfected. The lorry attached to the Section was engaged throughout the month in taking clothing from the laundries to the drying bath-houses and in moving the Section equipment to & from the various areas occupied by the Division.	
			F. S. Carson. Capt.	

Section 10
2nd London Sanitary Co RAMC,T. –
7th DIVISION –
B.E. Force. –
FRANCE –

140/1788

CONFIDENTIAL.

Vol III

10th Sanitary Section

Oct 1916

WAR DIARY
~ Vol. 3. ~

from 1st October 1916 to 31st October 1916

COMMITTEE FOR THE
MEDICAL HISTORY OF THE WAR

Date   -2 DEC. 1916

WAR DIARY or INTELLIGENCE SUMMARY

Army Form C. 2118.

Place	Date	Hour	Summary of Events and Information	Remarks and references to Appendices
PONT DE NEIPPE	1.10.16		Routine inspections of the Divisional area were continued. The sanitation & scavenging of NEIPPE were carried on & civilian labour supervised. The unit billeted in the area provided a squad of men for street sweeping under the supervision of an N.C.O. from the section. The various sources of water supply were visited & tests made for the amount of chlorine to be added - several supply posts were numbered & notice boards fixed. Incinerators are being built at NEIPPE & at the 7th Division camp at PAPOT (B.3d q.2 sheet 36 France) by men attached to the section. An N.C.O. of the section was sent to the Divl. Gas School for instruction in testing the new pattern box respirators. Lieut Miller of the 23rd Field Ambulance was attached to the Sanitary Section for a short course of instruction in Military Hygiene. N.C.O's and men of the 91st Field Co. R.E, 171st Field Coy, 35 Pontoon Park, & 9th Entrenching Battn	

WAR DIARY
or
INTELLIGENCE SUMMARY.

(Erase heading not required.)

Army Form C. 2118.

Instructions regarding War Diaries and Intelligence Summaries are contained in F. S. Regs., Part II. and the Staff Manual respectively. Title pages will be prepared in manuscript.

Hour, Date, Place	Summary of Events and Information	Remarks and references to Appendices
PONT. DE NEIPPE 1. 10. 16	Routine inspections of the Divisional area were continued The sanitation & scavenging of NEIPPE were carried on & civilian labour supervised. The unit billeted in the area provided a squad of men for street sweeping under the supervision of an NCO from the section. The various sources of water supply were visited & tests made for the amount of chlorine to be added - several supply posts were numbered & notice boards fixed. Incinerators are being built at NEIPPE & at the 7th Division camp at PAPOT (B.3.d 92 sheet 36 France) by men attached to the section. An N.C.O. of the section was sent to the Divl Gas School for instruction in testing the new pattern box respirators. Pint Miller of the 23rd Field Ambulance was attached to the Sanitary Section for a short course of instruction in Military Hygiene. N.C.O's and men of the 91st Field Coy R.E, 171st Field Coy R.E, No 2 Pontoon Park & 9th Entrenching Battn	

(73989) W4141—463. 400,000. 9/14. H.&J.Ltd. Forms/C. 2118/10.

Place	Date	Hour	Summary of Events and Information	Remarks and references to Appendices
			were bathed at PONT-DE-NEIPPE and 196th Field Coy R.E. at PAPOT. Laundry & disinfection work were continued. The N.C.O. of the Section who had been left in charge of the clothing at ARMENTIÈRES returned to the section & reported that the clothing had been removed by No 50 Supply Column. F.S. Carson Capt. R.A.M.C.	
PONT-DE-NEIPPE	2/10/16		Routine inspections of the Divisional area were carried on by the inspectors of the section. The sanitation & supervision of civilian labour in NEIPPE &c were continued. Water tests were made & patrols visited. I inspected the areas occupied by the Heavy Trench Mortar battery at D.20.c sheet 28, and also the billets vacated by No 4 Siege Coy R.E. at T.30.c.8.8 sheet 28 and reported upon their unsatisfactory condition to the A.D.M.S. of the 7th Division. A list shewing the type of latrine used by units in the Divisional area was sent to the A.D.M.S. The N.C.O's & men of the section were instructed in the use of the new	

WAR DIARY
or
INTELLIGENCE SUMMARY
(Erase heading not required.)

Army Form C. 2118.

Instructions regarding War Diaries and Intelligence Summaries are contained in F. S. Regs., Part II. and the Staff Manual respectively. Title Pages will be prepared in manuscript.

Place	Date	Hour	Summary of Events and Information	Remarks and references to Appendices
			pattern box respirator. Public latrines & incinerators are being erected in the NEIPPE area N.C.O's & men of the 8th Devons were bathed at PONT-DE-NEIPPE, the 2nd R. Irish & Dwn Train at POPOT. and 20th Manchesters at "The Piggeries" U.19 c 2 8 sheet 28. Soiled clothing received at the bath houses was disinfected. The case of Dysentery No 32026 Pte Bolton of the 1st Welch Fus attached to the 22nd Bgde T.M Battery was investigated with a view to finding a possible carrier. I reported at the A.D.M.S's office at 10 a.m. F. S. Carson Capt R.A.M.C.T	
PONT-DE NEIPPE	3/10/16		Routine inspections were continued & the sanitation &c of the NEIPPE area carried on. Public latrines & incinerators are being built in the NEIPPE area. I inspected the village of LE BIZET (C 13 b & d sheet 36) the areas occupied by the 20th Bgde M Gun Coy & T.M Battery and also the 2nd Gordons	

2449 Wt. W14957/M90 750,000 1/16 J.B.C. & A. Forms/C.2118/12.

WAR DIARY
or
INTELLIGENCE SUMMARY
(Erase heading not required.)

Army Form C. 2118.

Instructions regarding War Diaries and Intelligence Summaries are contained in F. S. Regs., Part II. and the Staff Manual respectively. Title Pages will be prepared in manuscript.

Place	Date	Hour	Summary of Events and Information	Remarks and references to Appendices
PONT DE NEIPPE	4/10/16		Water patrols & water testing were continued & several new notice boards fixed on the supply posts. The case of suspected Dysentery No 18373 Pte Cooper of the 8th Devons was investigated. The N.C.O. of the section who had been supervising the sanitation of the "Rest Camp" at AULT returned to the section. N.C.O's & men of the 20th Bgde Pioneer Platoon were bathed at PONT DE NEIPPE — the 11th Labour Battn R.E., 2nd Royal Irish Regt., Div'l Signals, M. Gun Coy and 14th Bgde R.H.A. at PAPOT and the 2nd Queens at The Piggeries. Disinfection of clothing was continued. J.S. CAVEN Capt. R.A.M.C.T. I inspected several water supply posts in the Divisional area & also visited the C.C. IX Corps Water Patrols office & A.D.M.S's office. Lieut Nowell was attached to the Sanitary Section for a short course of instruction in Military Hygiene. Routine inspections were continued in the Divisional area	

WAR DIARY
or
INTELLIGENCE SUMMARY
(Erase heading not required.)

Army Form C. 2118.

Instructions regarding War Diaries and Intelligence Summaries are contained in F. S. Regs., Part II. and the Staff Manual respectively. Title Pages will be prepared in manuscript.

Place	Date	Hour	Summary of Events and Information	Remarks and references to Appendices
			The sanitation & scavenging of the NEIPPE area was supervised.	
			Water patrols were visited & water tests made.	
			The following cases of Dysentery were investigated with a view to finding a possible carrier. N. 53064 Pte Lovell, 35th Bgde R.F.A., & N. 2504 Pte Lynch, 2nd Queens Regt — 2/Lieut Taylor who was notified as a case of Dysentery in the 1st South Staffords could not be traced in that Regiment	
			N.C.O's & men of the 24th Manchesters & 22nd Bgde R.F.A. were bathed at PONT DE NEIPPE — 2nd R. Warwicks, 7th Divnl Train & 22nd Bgde T.M. Battery at PAPOT and 1st R Welsh Fusileers at the Piggeries.	
			Laundry & disinfection work were carried on.	
			F. S. Carson Capt. R.A.M.C.-T.	
PONT. DE NEIPPE	5/10/16		I visited several water posts in the area.	
			Routine inspections were made by the inspectors of the section and the sanitation & scavenging of the NEIPPE area carried on.	
			An incinerator was being built at the 22nd Bgde camp at PAPOT.	

2449 Wt. W14957/M90 750,000 1/16 J.B.C. & A. Forms/C.2118/12.

WAR DIARY or INTELLIGENCE SUMMARY

Army Form C. 2118.

Place	Date	Hour	Summary of Events and Information	Remarks and references to Appendices
			Lieut Miller R.A.M.C. who was attached to the Sanitary Section on 1.10.16 returned to the 23rd Field Ambulance. NCO's & men of the 8th Devons - 7th Divl Amm. Column, 21st Manchesters & 7th Divl Artillery were bathed at PONT-DE-NEIPPE - the 2nd Royal Warwicks, 11th Labour Batt. R.E., & 7th Divl Artillery at PAPOT and the 1st R. Welch Fusiliers & 91st Bgde Grenade Coy at "THE PIGGERIES" Laundry & Disinfection work were continued. F.S. Carson Capt. R.A.M.C.	
PONT-DE-NEIPPE	6/10/16		I inspected the areas occupied by the 3rd Durham Field Coy R.E. and The Piggeries bath house and also made enquiries about the case of Brig Gen. Ford 91st Inf Bgde who was sent to hospital as a case of suspected Enteric fever. Routine inspections were continued by the inspectors of the section and the sanitation and scavenging of the NEIPPE area supervised. Water patrols were visited & tests made for the amount of chlorine to be	

WAR DIARY
or
INTELLIGENCE SUMMARY
(Erase heading not required.)

Army Form C. 2118.

Instructions regarding War Diaries and Intelligence Summaries are contained in F. S. Regs., Part II. and the Staff Manual respectively. Title Pages will be prepared in manuscript.

Place	Date	Hour	Summary of Events and Information	Remarks and references to Appendices
			added at several supply posts.	

Brick Incinerators are being built at PAPOT. (8 3 d 9.2. sheet 36 France)

The billet occupied by Bg. Gen. Ford, 91st Inf Bgde, was washed out with cresol & spayed with a solution of formalin.

The case of Dysentery No 88693 Driver Wingrove, 22nd Bgde R Fd was investigated with a view to finding a possible "carrier".

N.C.O's and men of the 8th Devons, 7th Divn artillery & 2x th Manchesters were bathed at PONT-DE-NEIPPE - 14th Bgde R.H.A. & 1st South Staffords at PAPOT and 21st Manchesters & 22nd Bgde M.G.Coy at The Piggeries -

Laundry & disinfection work was continued.

Laundresses at Pont de Neippe & civilians at Neippe were paid for the week's work.

F. S. Craven
Capt.
R.A.M.C.

2449 Wt. W14957/M90 750,000 1/16 J.B.C. & A. Forms/C.2118/12.

WAR DIARY
or
INTELLIGENCE SUMMARY
(Erase heading not required.)

Army Form C. 2118.

Instructions regarding War Diaries and Intelligence Summaries are contained in F. S. Regs., Part II. and the Staff Manual respectively. Title Pages will be prepared in manuscript.

Place	Date	Hour	Summary of Events and Information	Remarks and references to Appendices
PONT. DE NEIPPE	7/10/16		I visited the water posts JESUS FARM (B 26 d 3 0 sheet 36) and P. EGSTEERT (U 26. sheet 36) and inspected the area occupied by the 22nd Bgde Transport. Inspections of the Divisional area were made by the inspectors of the section & the scavenging & sanitation of the NEIPPE area were continued. Water posts were visited & tests made. NCOs & men of 22nd & 35th Bgdes R.F.A. - 14th Bgde R.H.A, 171st Coy R.E, 20th Pioneer Platoon & 95th Coy R.E, were bathed at PONT DE NEIPPE and 1st South Staffords, 20th Manchesters and 11th Labour Battalion at PAPOT. Laundry & disinfection work were continued. Men of the section & attached men were paid. F. S. Carson, Capt. R.A.M.C-T.	
PONT. DE NEIPPE	8/10/16		I inspected the areas occupied by No 2 Coy- 7th Divl train & the "huts" at PAPOT (B 3 d sheet 36) and reported upon the verminous condition of the huts to the A.D.M.S. Routine inspections of the Divisional area were made & the sanitation &	

WAR DIARY
or
INTELLIGENCE SUMMARY
(Erase heading not required.)

Army Form C. 2118.

Instructions regarding War Diaries and Intelligence Summaries are contained in F. S. Regs., Part II. and the Staff Manual respectively. Title Pages will be prepared in manuscript.

Place	Date	Hour	Summary of Events and Information	Remarks and references to Appendices
			Scavenging of the NEIPPE area supervised by N.C.O's & men of the section.	
			Water testing & the supervision of water patrols were carried on.	
			The billet of No 7953 Pte Stark, 91st Bgde M.G. Coy, a case of suspected Enteric was disinfected with cresol & a solution of Formalin.	
			Enquiries were made into the case of suspected Enteric No 7719 Dr Nye. 32nd Bgde R.F.A. with a view to finding a possible "carrier".	
			The case of Dysentery No 167 Sergt Kilpatrick who was notified as being in the 22nd Bgde R.F.A. could not be traced in that unit.	
			On instructions received from 7th Divl Headquarters the 7 men of the 2nd R. Irish Regt attached to the section for water duties were returned to their unit.	
			N.C.O's & men of 2nd Border Regt, 9th Entrenching Bn & 21st Manchesters were bathed at PONT-DE-NEIPPE and 196th Coy R.E. & 91st Bgde M.G. Coy at PAPOT.	
			Laundry & disinfection work were continued.	
			F. S. Carson, Capt RAMC T	

2449 Wt. W14957/M90 750,000 1/16 J.B.C. & A. Forms/C.2118/12.

WAR DIARY or INTELLIGENCE SUMMARY

Army Form C. 2118.

Place	Date	Hour	Summary of Events and Information	Remarks and references to Appendices
PONT DE NEIPPE	9/10/16		I inspected the area occupied by the 1st South Staffords & interviewed the Medical Officer about 2 cases of suspected Typhoid in the unit. Routine inspections of the Divn^l area & the supervision of scavenging & sanitation of NEIPPE area were continued. An incinerator is being built at PAPOT by a man attached to the Section. Water testing & supervision of water patrols were continued. N.C.O's & men of the 171st Coy R.E., 2nd Border Regt, 4th Bde R.H.A. & No 50 Supply column were bathed at PONT-DE-NEIPPE, the 21st & 22nd Manchesters at PAPOT and 2nd Queens at "The Piggeries". F. S. Carson Capt.	
PONT. DE NEIPPE	10/10/16		I reported at the A.D.M.S.'s office at 10 a.m. and also interviewed the D.A.D.O.S, who visited the laundry at PONT-DE-NEIPPE, in reference to washing socks so that men in the trenches may have their socks changed each day. I inspected the 7th Division billets in PONT DE NEIPPE.	

WAR DIARY
or
INTELLIGENCE SUMMARY
(Erase heading not required.)

Army Form C. 2118.

Instructions regarding War Diaries and Intelligence Summaries are contained in F. S. Regs., Part II. and the Staff Manual respectively. Title Pages will be prepared in manuscript.

Place	Date	Hour	Summary of Events and Information	Remarks and references to Appendices
			Lieut Nowell who had been attached to the Sanitary Section returned to the 23rd Field Ambulance.	
			Routine inspections were continued by the inspectors of the Section in the Dvn area.	
			The sanitation & scavenging of the NEIPPE area were continued.	
			Water testing was carried on & the patrols visited.	
			A scheme for the clarification of the sullage water at "the Piggeries" bath house was commenced.	
			N C O s & men of 2nd Border Regt 11th Bgde R. H. A, and No 50 Supply Column were bathed at PONT DE NEIPPE and the 20th Manchesters & 7th Divl train at PAPOT.	
			Laundry work & disinfection of clothing were continued.	
			F. S. Cason Capt same T	
PONT DE NEIPPE	11/10/16		I visited the D A D O S's office for further information in regard to a daily change of socks for men in the trenches	
			I inspected the area occupied by the 20th Manchesters and visited	

2449 Wt. W14957/M90 750,000 1/16 J.B.C. & A. Forms/C.2118/12.

WAR DIARY or INTELLIGENCE SUMMARY

Army Form C. 2118.

Place	Date	Hour	Summary of Events and Information	Remarks and references to Appendices
			PAPOT bath house. The inspectors of the section continued their inspections of the Div'l area and the sanitation of the NEIPPE area was carried on. Water tests were made & the water patrols visited. A plan shewing the Divisional area and the positions of the various water supply points was made & sent to the A.D.M.S. Cpl Bates & Pte Fallows reported to the section as reinforcements. NCO's & men of the 14th Bgde R.F.A., "L" Coy R.E. & 24th Manchesters were bathed at PONT-DE-NEIPPE and the 20th Manchesters & 7th Div'l Train at PAPOT. Laundry work & disinfection of clothing were continued. F. S. Carson, Capt. RAMC-T	
PONT DE NEIPPE	12/10/16		I inspected the areas occupied by the Anti-aircraft section, the Traffic police at NEIPPE (B.9.d. sheet 36) and 509th Howitzer Battery att'd to 101st Bgde R.F.A. Routine inspections were made by the inspectors of the section. Sanitation & scavenging of the NEIPPE area were supervised.	

WAR DIARY
or
INTELLIGENCE SUMMARY
(Erase heading not required.)

Army Form C. 2118.

Instructions regarding War Diaries and Intelligence Summaries are contained in F. S. Regs., Part II. and the Staff Manual respectively. Title Pages will be prepared in manuscript.

Place	Date	Hour	Summary of Events and Information	Remarks and references to Appendices
			Water tests were made & patrols visited.	
			N.C.O's & men of 2nd Border Regt, Canadian A.S.C., and 24th Manchesters were bathed at PONT-DE NEIPPE – 11th Labour Battn & 91st Bgde M.G. Coy at PAPOT and 21st Manchesters at "The Piggeries"	
			Laundry work & disinfection of clothing were continued.	
			F. S. Carson Capt R.A.M.C.–T.	
PONT DE NEIPPE	13/10/16		I inspected the PLOEGSTEERT wood area and the billets occupied by the 2nd R. Warwicks & 2nd R. Warwicks bombers & also the 22nd Bgde M.G. Coy.	
			I reported at the A.D.M.S.'s office at 3 p.m.	
			Routine inspections and the supervision of sanitation were continued in the Divisional area.	
			Water tests were made & the sources of supply visited.	
			The case of Dysentery No 98665 Pte Frith of the 22nd Bgde R.F.A. was investigated with a view to finding a possible "carrier"	
			N.C.O's & men of the 7th Divl Artillery, 171st & 95th Coys R.E. 20th Bgde	

2449 Wt. W14957/M90 750,000 1/16 J.B.C. & A. Forms/C.2118/12.

WAR DIARY
or
INTELLIGENCE SUMMARY
(Erase heading not required.)

Army Form C. 2118.

Place	Date	Hour	Summary of Events and Information	Remarks and references to Appendices
			Pioneer Platoon, 2nd Border Regt, 24th Manchesters & No 50 Supply Column were bathed at PONT-DE-NEIPPE, and the 1st R. Welsh Fus., 22nd Bde Grenade Coy & T.M. Battery and the 7th Divnl Train at PAPOT. Laundry & disinfection work were continued. Civilians employed for laundry & scavenging work were paid. F. S. Carson, Capt R.A.M.C.-T.	
PONT-DE-NEIPPE	14/10/16		I inspected the area occupied by the 22nd Manchesters, 21st Manchesters Bombers and the "Red Lodge" area (T.18d sheet 28) and visited the water supply posts. The cases of Dysentery, No 43055 Pte Parker of the 21st Field Ambulance, No 9172 Pte Dodd, 1st South Staffords and No 19771 Pte Rellford of the 8th Devons were investigated with a view to finding possible "carriers". Routine inspections were made in the Divnl area & the sanitation of the NEIPPE area supervised. NCOs & men of the 95th Coy RE, 2nd Gordons, 24th Manchesters & 20th	

WAR DIARY
or
INTELLIGENCE SUMMARY
(Erase heading not required.)

Army Form C. 2118.

Instructions regarding War Diaries and Intelligence Summaries are contained in F. S. Regs., Part II. and the Staff Manual respectively. Title Pages will be prepared in manuscript.

Place	Date	Hour	Summary of Events and Information	Remarks and references to Appendices
			Brigade T.M. Battery were bathed at PONT-DE-NEIPPE – 2nd Queens, 1st R. Welsh Fusileers & 11th Labour Battn at PAPOT and the Australian R.E's at "The Piggeries". Laundry & Disinfection work were continued – J.S. Carson, Capt RAMC _T	
PONT. DE. NEIPPE	15/10/16		I inspected the NEIPPE area & also visited several water supply posts. Routine inspections were made in the Divisional area & the sanitation & scavenging of NEIPPE continued – A brick incinerator is being built at PONT DE NEIPPE and the latrines at the PONT DE NEIPPE laundry made flyproof. The billet of No 5108 Sergt. Westwood. R.A.M.C 23rd F Ambulance was disinfected. this was a case of suspected Diphtheria. N.C.O's men of the 7th Divl Signals, 7th Labour Bn. 9th Entrenching Bn & 2nd Pontoon Park R.E's. the 7th Divl. Artillery and 2nd Border Regiment were bathed at PONT-DE-NEIPPE – and the 11th Labour Battn	

2449 Wt. W14957/M90 750,000 1/16 J.B.C. & A. Forms/C.2118/12.

WAR DIARY
or
INTELLIGENCE SUMMARY
(Erase heading not required.)

Army Form C. 2118.

Instructions regarding War Diaries and Intelligence Summaries are contained in F. S. Regs., Part II. and the Staff Manual respectively. Title Pages will be prepared in manuscript.

Place	Date	Hour	Summary of Events and Information	Remarks and references to Appendices
			and 1st R. Welsh Fusileers at "The Piggeries". Disinfection of clothing was continued. F.S. Carson, Capt. R.A.M.C._T	
PONT DE NEIPPE	16/10/16		I inspected the water supply points in PLOEGSTEERT wood. Routine inspections & sanitation in the Divnl area were continued. Water tests were made & patrols visited. The inspectors of the section also visited the Estaminets in the Divnl area to see that the Second Army order re-cleansing of drinking glasses, was being carried out. The case of suspected Erysipelas No 10014 Pte G. Smith - 3rd Gordon Hdrs. was investigated & the billet disinfected. The building of the incinerator at NEIPPE was continued & the latrines at the laundry made fly proof. NCO's & men of the 7th Divnl Artillery, 171st Coy R.E. & 2nd Border Regt were bathed at PONT-DE-NEIPPE _ 2nd Hon Artillery 6th and 7th	

WAR DIARY
or
INTELLIGENCE SUMMARY

(Erase heading not required.)

Army Form C. 2118.

Instructions regarding War Diaries and Intelligence Summaries are contained in F. S. Regs., Part II. and the Staff Manual respectively. Title Pages will be prepared in manuscript.

Place	Date	Hour	Summary of Events and Information	Remarks and references to Appendices
PONT DE NEIPPE	17/10/16		Divisional train at PAPOT and 24th Manchesters at The Piggeries. Laundry & Disinfection work were continued - F.S. Carson, Capt RAMC T The inspectors of the section continued visiting the Estaminets in the Div'l area re the cleaning of drinking glasses. Routine sanitation in the NEIPPE area was carried on The incinerator at PONT DE NEIPPE & the latrines at the laundry were proceeded with - NCOs men of the 2nd Queens & 11th Labour Batt'n were bathed at at PAPOT Laundry & Disinfection work were continued. 987 blankets from the 2nd Border Regt were disinfested F.S. Carson, Capt RAMC T	

2449 Wt. W14957/M90 750,000 1/16 J.B.C. & A. Forms/C.2118/12.

WAR DIARY or INTELLIGENCE SUMMARY

Army Form C. 2118.

Place	Date	Hour	Summary of Events and Information	Remarks and references to Appendices
PONT DE NEIPPE	18/10/16		I visited the PAPOT bath house & inspected the area occupied by 2 y T.M. Battery, 22nd Byde Signals & Cinder Farm. Routine inspections & sanitation were carried on. Water tests were made & notice boards fixed. N.C.O.'s & men of 2nd Gordons & 24th Manchesters were bathed at PONT DE NEIPPE - 2nd H.A.C. at PAPOT and Australian R.E.'s at the Piggeries. Laundry & Disinfection work was continued. F.S. Carson, Capt RAMC	
PONT DE NEIPPE	19/10/16		I visited the water supply posts in the Divisional area. Routine inspections & the supervision of scavenging were continued. Water tests were made & notice boards fixed. N.C.O's & men of 171st & 95th Coy R.E's & 7th Dvnl Artillery were bathed at PONT DE NEIPPE and the 11th Labour Battn, 1st South Stafford's, 91st Byde Hqrs	

WAR DIARY
or
INTELLIGENCE SUMMARY
(Erase heading not required.)

Army Form C. 2118.

Instructions regarding War Diaries and Intelligence Summaries are contained in F. S. Regs., Part II. and the Staff Manual respectively. Title Pages will be prepared in manuscript.

Place	Date	Hour	Summary of Events and Information	Remarks and references to Appendices
			22ⁿᵈ Manchesters, "F" Battery R.H.A. and 21ˢᵗ Manchesters at PAPOT.	
			Disinfection of clothing & the laundry work were continued —	
			F. S. Carson, Capt. R.A.M.C.-T	
PONT. DE NEIPPE	20/10/16		I inspected the areas occupied by the 19ᵗʰ Heavy Artillery Group H.Qrs. 90ᵗʰ Siege Battery R.G.A., & 176ᵗʰ Battery R.G.A.	
			Inspections of the Divᵒⁿˡ area were made by the inspectors of the section in the various sub-areas.	
			The sanitation & scavenging of the NEIPPE area were continued —	
			A new pattern incinerator for burning excreta was commenced at the PONT-DE-NEIPPE laundry.	
			Water tests were made & patrols visited —	
			N.C.O.'s & men of 9ᵗʰ Devons, & 7ᵗʰ Divᵒⁿ Artillery were bathed at PONT DE-NEIPPE & 2ⁿᵈ Gordons, 22ⁿᵈ Bgde M.G.Coy & 7ᵗʰ Divᵒⁿ train at PAPOT.	
			Disinfection of clothing & laundry work were continued —	
			Laundresses & civilian scavengers were paid for the weeks work	
			F. S. Carson, Capt. R.A.M.C.-T	

WAR DIARY
or
INTELLIGENCE SUMMARY
(Erase heading not required.)

Army Form C. 2118.

Instructions regarding War Diaries and Intelligence Summaries are contained in F. S. Regs., Part II. and the Staff Manual respectively. Title Pages will be prepared in manuscript.

Place	Date	Hour	Summary of Events and Information	Remarks and references to Appendices
PONT DE NIEPPE	21/10/16		I visited the water supply posts at Reserve Farm (C.3.d.6.0 sheet 36) Dispierre Farm (C.3.c.7.6 sheet 36) & Lancashire Farm (U.27.b.3.1 sheet 36) and inspected the middle sector of the trenches & 2nd Border Regt billets at LE BIZET. Routine inspections of the Divisional area were made by the inspectors of the section. The scavenging & sanitation in the NIEPPE area were carried out. Water tests were made & notice boards fixed. N.C.Os & men of the 1st Divnl Artillery & 23rd Field Amb were bathed at PONT DE-NIEPPE and the Australian R.E's, 21st Field Amb & 1st Lgt de Grenade Coy at The Piggeries. Laundry work & disinfection of clothing were carried on. Men of the Section & attached men were paid. F.S. Carson, Capt RAMC T.	
PONT DE NIEPPE	22/10/16		I visited the A.D.M.S's office & inspected the sanitary arrangements in the NIEPPE area. Routine inspections were continued in the Divisional area.	

WAR DIARY
or
INTELLIGENCE SUMMARY

(Erase heading not required.)

Army Form C. 2118.

Instructions regarding War Diaries and Intelligence Summaries are contained in F. S. Regs., Part II. and the Staff Manual respectively. Title Pages will be prepared in manuscript.

Place	Date	Hour	Summary of Events and Information	Remarks and references to Appendices
			Water tests were made & the patrols visited - N.C.O's & men of 7th Divnl Signals, 171st Coy R.E., 7 Labour Battn, 9th Entrenching Bn, 2nd Pontoon Park & 35th Siege Battery were bathed at PONT DE NEIPPE. 2nd Manchesters & 11th Labour Battn at PAPOT and 1st South Staffords at The Piggeries The disinfector could not be used owing to damages caused in preparing for an inspection by an officer attached to Second Army - An extra shed for washing socks at the NEIPPE laundry is in course of construction - F. S. Caesar Capt.	
PONT. DE. NEIPPE	23/10/16		I visited the A.D.M.S. office, the office of the D.D. II Corps Water patrols and also interviewed the 9th Division S.S.O. re-coal for laundry work. I inspected the water supply points at BRUNE GAYE (B.10a sheet 36) and PAPOT (B.9b sheet 36) Routine inspections were continued by the section inspectors The sanitation & scavenging of the NEIPPE area were continued - Water tests were made & patrols visited -	

2449 Wt. W14957/M90 750,000 1/16 J.B.C. & A. Forms/C.2118/12.

WAR DIARY
or
INTELLIGENCE SUMMARY
(Erase heading not required.)

Army Form C. 2118.

Place	Date	Hour	Summary of Events and Information	Remarks and references to Appendices
PONT DE NEIPPE	24/10/16		N.C.O's and men of the 7th Divl. Artillery, 56th Supply Column & 20th Bgde T.M. Battery were bathed at PONT-DE-NEIPPE. 2nd R. Warwicks, 22nd Bgde Grenade Coy & Divnl Train at PAPOT, and 1st R. Welsh Fus. & 91st Brigade T.M. Battery at "The Piggeries". The repairs to the disinfector were completed by men from No 56 Supply Column. Laundry work was continued. The men on water duties were paid. F. S. Carson. Capt RAMC-T I inspected the right sector of the trenches occupied by the Division and the water supplies at LE TOUQUET STATION (C 9d sheet 36) I reported at the A.D.M.S. office at 3.30 pm. Inspections of the Divisional area were made by the inspectors of the section. The sanitation & scavenging in the NEIPPE area were continued. A new brick incinerator was commenced at the ROMARIN camp (B.4c. sheet 36)	

Place	Date	Hour	Summary of Events and Information	Remarks and references to Appendices

Water tests were made & supply posts inspected.

N.C.O's & men of the 9th Devons & 7th Div. Ammn Column were bathed at PONT DE-NEIPPE - the 11th Labour Bn, 91st M.G. Coy and 22nd Manchesters at PAPOT and 1st South Staffords at The Piggeries.

Laundry work & disinfection of clothing were continued -

F. S. Carson, Capt R.A.M.C.-T.

PONT DE NEIPPE   25/10/16

I inspected the ROMARIN camp (B.4.c. sheet 36) and visited the bath-house at PAPOT.

Routine inspections were made in the Divl area & the sanitation & scavenging of the NEIPPE area supervised.

Water testing was continued & the patrols visited.

The case of suspected Diphtheria No 9038 Pte W. Kirton. 2nd Border Regt. was investigated & the billet disinfected.

N.C.O's & men of 171st & 95th Coys R.E., 20th Byde T.M.B & Pioneer Platoon and 50th Supply Column were bathed at PONT DE-NEIPPE - the 20th

WAR DIARY or INTELLIGENCE SUMMARY

Army Form C. 2118.

(Erase heading not required.)

Place	Date	Hour	Summary of Events and Information	Remarks and references to Appendices
			20th Manchesters at PSPOT and the 2nd H.AC, Canadian R.E and 91st Bgde T.M.B at The Piggeries. Disinfection & Laundry work were continued. F. S. Carson, Cap RAMC T	
PONT DE NEIPPE	26/10/16		I inspected billets in the NEIPPE area & visited the 7th Divl School. Interviewed the 25th Divn Sanitary Officer & 7th Divn D.A.D.O.S. re clothing to be exchanged with the 25th Division. Reported at the A.D.M.S. at 10 a.m. Routine inspections were carried on. Sanitation & scavenging in the NEIPPE area were continued. The case of Dysentery No 13381 Dvr O'Keefe - 7th Divl Amn Col. was investigated. Water tests were made & patrols supervised. Investigations were made regarding a case of Measles (Marthi Desfrance) amongst the Civilian population at 5.30. a 10.2 Sheet 28. N.C.O's & men of the 8th Devons, 7th Divl Artillery & 23rd Field Ambulance	

WAR DIARY
or
INTELLIGENCE SUMMARY
(Erase heading not required.)

Army Form C. 2118.

Instructions regarding War Diaries and Intelligence Summaries are contained in F. S. Regs., Part II. and the Staff Manual respectively. Title Pages will be prepared in manuscript.

Place	Date	Hour	Summary of Events and Information	Remarks and references to Appendices
PONT DE NEIPPE	27/10/16		were bathed at PONT DE-NEIPPE – 11th Labour Bn 22nd Brigade M.G. Coy & T.M. Bat and Grenade Coy, 1st R. Welsh Fus. and 2nd A. Art. Coy at P.?POT and the 91st Bgde Grenade Coy & Australian R.E. at The Piggeries. Disinfection work & Laundry work were carried on –	
			F. S. Carson, Capt. R.A.M.C _T.	
			Routine inspections were made in the Divisional area by the inspectors of the section – Lieut Giblin, 22nd F. Amb., was attached to the section for a short course of Military Hygiene. Two N.C.O.'s of the section were sent to BEAUVAL to see the method of sanitation that is being carried out in the area & obtain particulars of the Laundry. Water testing was continued & patrols inspected. The sanitation & scavenging of the NEIPPE area were continued – N.C.O.s & men of the 8th Devons and 2nd M.D.C. were bathed at PONT DE-NEIPPE – the 20th Manchesters & ? Divl train at P?POT and the	

WAR DIARY or INTELLIGENCE SUMMARY

Army Form C. 2118.

Place	Date	Hour	Summary of Events and Information	Remarks and references to Appendices
PONT-DE-NEIPPE	28/10/16		Australian R.E.'s at the Piggeries. Disinfection & laundry work were continued. F. S. Carson, Capt R.A.M.C.-T. I inspected the billets in PONT-DE-NEIPPE. Routine inspections of the Divl area were made & the sanitation in the NEIPPE area supervised. Water tests were made & notice boards fixed. N.C.O.'s & men of the 171st Coy R.E., 50th Supply Column, Canadian C.C.S., & 2nd Gordons were bathed at PONT-DE-NEIPPE and the 91st Bde Grenade Coy & Drainage Coy at "The Piggeries". Laundry work & disinfection of clothing were continued. F. S. Carson Capt R.A.M.C.-T.	

WAR DIARY
or
INTELLIGENCE SUMMARY
(Erase heading not required.)

Army Form C. 2118.

Instructions regarding War Diaries and Intelligence Summaries are contained in F. S. Regs., Part II. and the Staff Manual respectively. Title Pages will be prepared in manuscript.

Place	Date	Hour	Summary of Events and Information	Remarks and references to Appendices
PONT. DE NEIPPE	29/10/16		Routine inspections of the sanitation carried out by units in the dwl. area were made.	
			The sanitation & scavenging of the NIEPPE were continued.	
			Water testing & supervision of water patrols were carried on.	
			The cases of Dysentery T/24216 Pte. McKenney, A.S.C. attd 21st Field Amb, and Sergt Hamilton (No 5155) 10th attd 2nd Gordons were enquired into — the latter case was not found in the 7th Division —	
			N.C.O's & men of the 8th Devons, 9th Entrenching Battn, 7th Divl Signals, 7th Labour Battn & 7th Div artillery were bathed at PONT DE NEIPPE, the 11th Labour Battn, 91st Bgde M.G. Coy. & 1st South Staffords at ROOT, and the Australian R.Es at "The Piggeries —	
			Disinfection of clothing was continued	
			F. S. Cannon, Capt R.A.M.C_T.	

2449 Wt. W14957/M90 750,000 1/16 J.B.C. & A. Forms/C.2118/12.

WAR DIARY or INTELLIGENCE SUMMARY

Army Form C. 2118.

(Erase heading not required.)

Place	Date	Hour	Summary of Events and Information	Remarks and references to Appendices
PONT DE NEIPPE	30/10/16		I inspected the water supply posts in the PLOEGSTEERT wood area. Routine inspections were continued in the Divisional area & the scavenging of PONT-DE-NEIPPE carried on. Water supply posts were patrolled & tests made. NCO's & men of the 54th Coy R.E's & 23rd Bgde R.F.A. were bathed at PONT-DE-NEIPPE and the 1st R. Welsh Fus. at PAPOT. Laundry & disinfection work were continued. J. S. Carson, Capt RAMC-T.	
PONT DE NEIPPE	31/10/16		I reported at the A.D.M.S's office at 10 am and inspected the Bath House & laundry at PONT-DE-NEIPPE. Routine inspections of the sanitation in the Divisional area were continued.	

WAR DIARY
or
INTELLIGENCE SUMMARY
(Erase heading not required.)

Army Form C. 2118.

Instructions regarding War Diaries and Intelligence Summaries are contained in F. S. Regs., Part II. and the Staff Manual respectively. Title Pages will be prepared in manuscript.

Place	Date	Hour	Summary of Events and Information	Remarks and references to Appendices
			Water tests were made & the patrols inspected.	
			N.C.O's & men of 171st & 95th Coys R.B's - 7th Dvn artillery, 21st & 23rd Field	
			Ambulances and also the 8th Bn of North Lancashires, 9th Cheshires & N.3	
			Coy of the 25th Division were bathed at PONT. DE. NEIPPE - the 11th Labour	
			Battn & 1st South Staffords at PAPOT and the 2nd Queens at "The Piggeries"	
			Laundry work & disinfection of clothing were continued.	
			150 blankets belonging to the 11th Bgde R.H.A. were disinfected	
			Men of the section & all attached men were paid—	
			F.S. Carson, Capt R.A.M.C. T.	

2449 Wt. W14957/M90 750,000 1/16 J.B.C. & A. Forms/C.2118/12.

Nov 1916

140/846

No 10 Sanitary Sec[tion]

CONFIDENTIAL

Section
2nd London Sanitary Co R.A.M.C., T.
7th Division
B.E. Force - France.

Vol 4

Nov 1916

War Diary

Vol 4.

from 1st November 1916 to 30th November 1916.

COMMITTEE FOR THE
MEDICAL HISTORY OF THE WAR
Date -3 JAN. 1917

WAR DIARY
or
INTELLIGENCE SUMMARY

(Erase heading not required.)

Army Form C. 2118.

Instructions regarding War Diaries and Intelligence Summaries are contained in F. S. Regs., Part II. and the Staff Manual respectively. Title Pages will be prepared in manuscript.

Place	Date	Hour	Summary of Events and Information	Remarks and references to Appendices
PONT. DE. NEIPPE	1/11/16		Routine inspections were continued throughout the Divisional area. The sanitation & scavenging of NEIPPE was carried on. Water tests were made & the several water supply posts visited. Lieut Giblin who had been attached to the Sanitary Section for a short course of instruction in Military Hygiene returned to the 22ⁿ Field Ambulance. N.C.O's & men of the 7th Division Artillery, 90th Bgde R.G.A, 77th Field Ambulance & 8th Devons were bathed at PONT-DE-NEIPPE and the 2nd Hon. Artillery Coy and 7th Divisional Train at PAPOT. The bath house at "the PIGGERIES" was dismantled. Laundry & disinfection work were continued. F. S. Carson, Capt.	
PONT DE NEIPPE	2/11/16		I visited the area of FLETRE to find suitable sites for bath-houses and laundry.	

WAR DIARY or INTELLIGENCE SUMMARY

Army Form C. 2118.

Instructions regarding War Diaries and Intelligence Summaries are contained in F. S. Regs., Part II. and the Staff Manual respectively. Title Pages will be prepared in manuscript.

(Erase heading not required.)

Place	Date	Hour	Summary of Events and Information	Remarks and references to Appendices
			Routine inspections of the Divisional area were continued by the Inspectors of the Section.	
			The Sanitation & Scavenging of the NEIPPE area were continued.	
			Water tests were made & supply posts inspected.	
			N.C.O.'s of the 11th Labour Battalion & 2nd H. Artillery Bty were bathed at PAPOT.	
			The bath-house equipment & clothing belonging to the 7th Division were moved from PAPOT to STEENWERCK (A.11.d.2.8. sheet 36)	
			Laundry work & Disinfection of clothing were continued.	
			F. S. Carson Capt.	
PONT-DE-NEIPPE	3/11/16		The bath-house & laundry at METEREN (X.20.d.8.2. sheet 27) was taken over by an N.C.O. of the Section.	
			The Section moved from PONT-DE-NEIPPE to FLETRE.	
			All men attached from Battalions to the Section for Sanitary & water duties were returned to their units.	

WAR DIARY
or
INTELLIGENCE SUMMARY

(Erase heading not required.)

Instructions regarding War Diaries and Intelligence Summaries are contained in F. S. Regs., Part II. and the Staff Manual respectively. Title Pages will be prepared in manuscript.

Army Form C. 2118.

Place	Date	Hour	Summary of Events and Information	Remarks and references to Appendices
PONT. DE NEIPPE	4/11/16		The Foden steam lorry (W.O. 5.318) was transferred to the Sanitary Section 25th Division. Laundry work was continued at PONT.-DE-NEIPPE. F. S. Carson. Capt. Section inspectors commenced their duties in the new area occupied by the Division. The case of Cerebro-Spinal-Meningitis (No 1363 Pte Fielding) in 2nd R. Warwicks was investigated with a view to finding a possible "carrier" All the clothing & equipment were moved from the laundry at PONT DE NEIPPE to the laundry at METEREN (X 20.d.8.2 sheet 27) and the bath house & laundry at PONT-DE-NEIPPE handed over to the Sanitary Officer 25th Division. The laundresses at PONT-DE-NEIPPE were paid for their work & told that they would not now be employed by the 7th Division. The Civilian scavengers were employed at NEIPPE were also paid off. and taken over by the 25th Division.	

2449 Wt. W14957/M90 750,000 1/16 J.B.C. & A. Forms/C.2118/12.

WAR DIARY
or
INTELLIGENCE SUMMARY
(Erase heading not required.)

Army Form C. 2118.

Instructions regarding War Diaries and Intelligence Summaries are contained in F. S. Regs., Part II. and the Staff Manual respectively. Title Pages will be prepared in manuscript.

Place	Date	Hour	Summary of Events and Information	Remarks and references to Appendices
			N.C.O's & men of the 20th Manchesters were bathed at STEENWERCK. F. S. Carson, Capt.	
FLETRE	5/11/16		Inspections of the sanitation of the Divisional area were continued. The sanitation & scavenging of the village of FLETRE was carried on. Water tests were made & notice boards fixed. N.C.O's & men of the 2nd Queens, 22nd Manchesters & 2nd New Zealand D.A.C. were bathed at METEREN. F. S. Carson, Capt.	
FLETRE	6/11/16		The inspectors of the Section continued their inspections of the Divisional area. A bath house was fitted up at CAESTRE. N.C.O's & men of 1st R. Welsh Fusileers were bathed at STEENWERCK and 2nd Border Regt & 22nd Manchester Regt. at METEREN. F. S. Carson, Capt.	

WAR DIARY
or
INTELLIGENCE SUMMARY

Army Form C. 2118.

Place	Date	Hour	Summary of Events and Information	Remarks and references to Appendices
FLETRE	7/11/16		Routine inspections & sanitation were continued in the area. The case of Diphtheria (No. 53601 Pte Stafforne) notified on in the R. Welsh Regt: could not be traced in the 114th Division. N.C.O. i/cs of 2nd Warwicks & 22nd Regtl Hdqrs: were billeted at STEENWERCK, 1st Stafford, 91st Bgde T.M. Battery & 2nd Queens at METEREN and 91st Bgde Headquarters at CAESTRE. Foundry work was commenced at METEREN. T.S. Cannon Capt.	
FLETRE	8/11/16		Routine inspections of the Bivouacs and area were continued – The 24th house at STEENWERCK, METEREN and CAESTRE were dismantled & all the clothing & equipment stored in a barn at FLETRE when an N.C.O. of the section was left in charge. The foundries employed at METEREN men found for the 2 days work. T.S. Cannon Capt.	

WAR DIARY or INTELLIGENCE SUMMARY

Army Form C. 2118.

Place	Date	Hour	Summary of Events and Information	Remarks and references to Appendices
FLETRE	9/11/16		The Sanitary section left FLETRE at 9 a.m. and marched to RENESCURE with Divisional Headquarters troops arriving at RENESCURE about 2 p.m. F.S. Carson Capt.	
RENESCURE	10/11/16		Section at RENESCURE awaiting further instructions. F.S. Carson Capt.	
RENESCURE	11/11/16		Section left RENESCURE at 9.30 a.m. & arrived at TILQUES about 2.30 p.m. F.S. Carson Capt.	
TILQUES	12/11/16		I visited various points in the Divisional area with the A.D.M.S. with the object of finding suitable places for bath houses. The case of Paratyphoid "B" (No. 12551 Pte Gamester) in the 2nd Royal Warwicks was investigated with a view to finding a possible carrier –	

WAR DIARY
or
INTELLIGENCE SUMMARY
(Erase heading not required.)

Army Form C. 2118.

Instructions regarding War Diaries and Intelligence Summaries are contained in F. S. Regs., Part II. and the Staff Manual respectively. Title Pages will be prepared in manuscript.

Place	Date	Hour	Summary of Events and Information	Remarks and references to Appendices
			The Foden steam lorry (W.O. Nº 330) with steam disinfector, transferred from the 25ᵗʰ Division, reported at TILQUES.	
			F. S. Carson Capt	
TILQUES	13/11/16		I visited Sᵗ Omer to make arrangements for washing the clothing handed in at the bath houses. Routine inspections of the Divisional area were made by the inspectors of the Section.	
			F. S. Carson Capt.	
TILQUES	14/11/16		Routine inspections were continued in the Divisional area. I visited WATTEN to interview the R.T.O. about the transport of clothing to the new area. The case of Suspected Diphtheria Nº 10761 Sergᵗ D Gardie of the 2ⁿᵈ Gordons was investigated with a view of finding a possible "carrier". The Bath house clothing was moved to the railhead at WATTEN.	
			F. S. Carson Capt.	

2449 Wt. W14957/M90 750,000 1/16 J.B.C. & A. Forms/C.2118/12.

WAR DIARY or INTELLIGENCE SUMMARY

(Erase heading not required.)

Army Form C. 2118.

Place	Date	Hour	Summary of Events and Information	Remarks and references to Appendices
TILQUES	15/11/16	9 a.m.	The Section moved with Divisional Hdqr troops to LUMBRES. F.S. Carson. Capt.	
LUMBRES	16/11/16	9.30 a.m.	The Section moved as yesterday to BOMY. F.S. Carson. Capt.	
BOMY	17/11/16		Section awaiting further movement orders. F.S. Carson. Capt.	
BOMY	18/11/16	9.10 a.m.	The Section moved with Divisional Hdqr troops to ANVIN F.S. Carson. Capt.	
ANVIN	19/11/16	9.45 a.m.	The Section moved as yesterday to FLERS F.S. Carson. Capt.	

WAR DIARY
or
INTELLIGENCE SUMMARY

(Erase heading not required.)

Army Form C. 2118.

Instructions regarding War Diaries and Intelligence Summaries are contained in F. S. Regs., Part II. and the Staff Manual respectively. Title Pages will be prepared in manuscript.

Place	Date	Hour	Summary of Events and Information	Remarks and references to Appendices
FLERS	20 11/16	9.45 a.m.	The Section moved as yesterday to FROHEN-LE-GRAND. J. S. Carson, Capt.	
FROHEN LE GRAND	21 11/16	9.30 a.m.	The Section moved as yesterday to DOULLENS J. S. Carson, Capt.	
DOULLENS	22 11/16		An N.C.O. of the Section was sent to get particulars of the bath house at MAILLY-MAILLET and another N.C.O. to BERTRANCOURT. The Section moved with Divisional Headquarter troops to MARIEUX. J. S. Carson, Capt.	
MARIEUX	23 11/16		I visited the A.D.M.S's office. Waiting for further movement orders. J. S. Carson, Capt.	
MARIEUX	24 11/16		N.C.O's of the Section were sent to take over the bath houses at MAILLY-MALLET, BERTRANCOURT, OCHEUX and MAILLY-MALLET WOOD (P.18 central sheet 57D) An N.C.O. and one man was sent to take over the laundry at AUTHIE and	

2449 Wt. W14957/M90 750,000 1/16 J.B.C. & A. Forms/C.2118/12.

WAR DIARY or INTELLIGENCE SUMMARY

(Erase heading not required.)

Army Form C. 2118.

Instructions regarding War Diaries and Intelligence Summaries are contained in F. S. Regs., Part II. and the Staff Manual respectively. Title Pages will be prepared in manuscript.

Place	Date	Hour	Summary of Events and Information	Remarks and references to Appendices
			obtain particulars of the clothing to be handed over by the 2nd Division. F. S. Carson Capt.	
MARIEUX	25/11/16	9.30 a.m.	The Section moved with Divisional Headquarters to BERTRANCOURT. Clothing was transferred from BEAUQUESNE to the bath houses at BERTRANCOURT and MAILLY-MAILLET. F. S. Carson Capt.	
BERTRANCOURT	26/11/16		I interviewed the Officer i/c 2nd Division Laundry at AUTHIE about the clothing to be handed over to the 7th Division. Clothing was transferred from BEAUQUESNES to the bath house at BERTRANCOURT bath house. N.C.O.'s & men of the 9th Devons were bathed at MAILLY-MALLET. The inspectors of the Section commenced their inspections in the new area occupied by the Division. F. S. Carson Capt.	

WAR DIARY
or
INTELLIGENCE SUMMARY
(Erase heading not required.)

Army Form C. 2118.

Instructions regarding War Diaries and Intelligence Summaries are contained in F. S. Regs., Part II. and the Staff Manual respectively. Title Pages will be prepared in manuscript.

Place	Date	Hour	Summary of Events and Information	Remarks and references to Appendices
BERTRANCOURT	27/11/16		Routine inspections were continued in the Divisional area.	
			Bath fittings were fitted up at MAILLY-MAILLET WOOD (P.13 central sheet 57d.)	
			N.C.O's & men of the 1st R.Welsh Fus were bathed at BERTRANCOURT.	
			Clean clothing was issued to men who were bathed.	
			Disinfection of clothing was done at the laundry at AUTHIE	
			The laundresses at BEAUQUESNES were paid for washing the clothing handed over to the 7th Division by the 25th Division.	
			F. S. Carson Capt	
BERTRANCOURT	28/11/16		I visited BOVES & made arrangements for having the Divisional clothing washed.	
			Routine inspections were made in the Divisional area by the inspectors of the Section.	
			One N.C.O. & one man were sent for duty at the XIIIth Corps Headquarters.	
			Two lorry loads of clean clothing were obtained from the XIIIth Corps laundry for the 7th Divn bath houses.	
			N.C.O's & men of 2nd R.Warwicks & 22nd Bgde M.Gun Coy were bathed at BERTRANCOURT.	
			2nd Gordons & 8th Devons at MAILLY-MAILLET WOOD and 8th Devon & 2nd Hon.Art.Coy	

2449 Wt. W14957/M90 750,000 1/16 J.B.C. & A. Forms/C.2118/12.

Place	Date	Hour	Summary of Events and Information	Remarks and references to Appendices
			at MAILLY-MALLET. Clean clothing was issued to all men who bathed. Disinfection of clothing was continued. F. S. Carson. Capt. R.A.M.C.-T.	
BERTRANCOURT	29/11/16		I visited the A.D.M.S's office & 7th Divn "Q" office to arrange about the transport of coal & clothing for the bath houses. The inspectors of the Section continued their inspections of the Divisional area. The bath house clothing & equipment was moved from the Rail head at VAUCHELLES to the laundry at AUTHIE. N.C.O's & men of the 20th Manchesters were bathed at BERTRANCOURT — 2nd Gordons & 2nd L. North Lancs at MAILLY WOOD and 2nd Gordons at MAILLY MAILLY. Clean clothing was issued — The disinfection of clothing was continued. Reports received from the inspectors of the Section show that the area taken over by the 7th Divn is in a very insanitary condition. F. S. Carson, Capt.	

			WAR DIARY *or* INTELLIGENCE SUMMARY	Army Form C. 2118.

Instructions regarding War Diaries and Intelligence Summaries are contained in F. S. Regs., Part II. and the Staff Manual respectively. Title Pages will be prepared in manuscript.

(Erase heading not required.)

Place	Date	Hour	Summary of Events and Information	Remarks and references to Appendices
BERTRANCOURT	30/11/16		Inspections of the Divisional Area were continued by the inspectors of the Section.	
			Water supplies were examined & tests made for the amount of chlorine to be added.	
			The bath. house at ACHEUX was handed over to the XIIIth Corps Hdqrs. and the men returned to their unit.	
			N.C.O's & men of the 2nd Queens 21st Manchesters - 12th L North Lancs - 91st Bgde T.M Battery - 91st Bgde Grenade Co. & 2nd Queens were bathed at MAILLY WOOD, 1st South Staffords & 22nd Manchesters at BERTRANCOURT and the 8th Devons & 20th Bgde Machine Gun Co. at MAILLY - MALLET.	
			Clothing from the bath. houses was disinfected.	
			An extra motor lorry was temporarily attached to the Section for the transport of clothing between the bath. houses & Laundries.	
			F. S. Carson. Capt.	
			The Section lorry was employed during the month in the transport of clothing for the bath. houses & also moving the Section equipment	

2449 Wt. W14957/M90 750,000 1/16 J.B.C. & A. Forms/C.2118/12.

WAR DIARY
or
INTELLIGENCE SUMMARY

(Erase heading not required.)

Army Form C. 2118.

Instructions regarding War Diaries and Intelligence Summaries are contained in F. S. Regs., Part II. and the Staff Manual respectively. Title Pages will be prepared in manuscript.

Place	Date	Hour	Summary of Events and Information	Remarks and references to Appendices

Dec. 1916

7th Div

140/1900

SECTION 10

2ⁿᵈ LONDON SANITARY COY. R.A.M.C. T.

B.E.F. _ FRANCE.

CONFIDENTIAL.

Vol 5

WAR DIARY.

VOL. 5.

1ˢᵗ DECEMBER 1916 TO 31ˢᵗ DECEMBER 1916.

COMMITTEE FOR THE
MEDICAL HISTORY OF THE WAR

Date   31 JAN. 1917

WAR DIARY or INTELLIGENCE SUMMARY.

Army Form C. 2118.

(Erase heading not required.)

Place	Date	Hour	Summary of Events and Information	Remarks and references to Appendices
BERTRANCOURT	1/12/16		I visited the laundry at AUTHIE I.17 & 1.7 sheet 57D and arranged with the Officer i/c for 2nd Division to take over the laundry for 7th Division. Routine inspections of the Divisional area were continued by the Sanitary Inspectors of the Section. Various water supply posts were inspected & chlorine tests made. Water carts were examined. N.C.O.'s & men of 22nd Manchesters, 1st South Staffords & 91st Brigade Machine Gun Coy were bathed at BERTRANCOURT. 21st Field Ambulance & 20th Brigade Machine Gun Coy at MAILLY-MAILLET and 2nd Queens & 21st Manchesters at P.18 central. Laundry work & disinfection of clothing were continued. The lorries attached to the Section took clothing to the bath-houses and laundries. F. S. Carson. Capt R.A.M.C.—T.	
BERTRANCOURT	2/12/16		Routine inspections of the Divisional area were carried out. New deep trench, fly proof box seat, public latrines are being made for the village	

WAR DIARY
or
INTELLIGENCE SUMMARY.

(Erase heading not required.)

Army Form C. 2118.

Instructions regarding War Diaries and Intelligence Summaries are contained in F. S. Regs., Part II. and the Staff Manual respectively. Title pages will be prepared in manuscript.

Place	Date	Hour	Summary of Events and Information	Remarks and references to Appendices
			of BERTRANCOURT to replace the present insanitary pail system — Water tests were made and several water carts examined — N.C.O's & men of 22nd Manchesters & 1st South Staffords were bathed at BERTRANCOURT, 9th Devons & 2nd Gordons at MAILLY-MAILLET and 2nd Horse Guards & 12th Loyal North Lancs at P.18 central — Laundry work & the disinfection of clothing were continued — No 1672 Pte N.E. Brown of this Section was sent sick, to the 23rd Field Ambulance —	
			F.S. Carson. Capt R.A.M.C-T.	
BERTRANCOURT	3/12/16		I inspected the sanitary arrangements of MAILLY-MAILLET, and the bath-houses at MAILLY-MAILLET and MAILLY WOOD (P.18 central) — Sanitation inspections were made in the Divisional area by the Inspectors of the Section. Water testing at various supply posts were made & water carts examined	

2353 Wt. W2544/1454 700,000 5/15 D. D. & L.   A.D.S.S./Forms/C. 2118.

WAR DIARY
or
INTELLIGENCE SUMMARY.

(Erase heading not required.)

Army Form C. 2118.

Place	Date	Hour	Summary of Events and Information	Remarks and references to Appendices
" "			New latrines are being proceeded with, for the village of BERTRANCOURT and "suggestions" for the organization of the sanitation of the village sent to the Town Commandant. NCO's & men of the 7th Divl. Signals Coy & 2nd H.A.C. were bathed at BERTRANCOURT, 2nd Borders & 9th Devons at MAILLY-MAILLET and 12th N.Lancs and 3rd Durham Field Coy. R.E's at P.18 central. Disinfection of clothing & laundry work were continued — F. S. Carson. Capt. R.A.M.C_T.	
BERTRANCOURT	4/12/16		I inspected the laundry at AUTHIE. Inspections of the sanitary arrangements in the Divisional area were continued — New latrines for BERTRANCOURT were proceeded with. Water testing was carried on — The case of Dysentery, No. 40766 Pte. Conway of the 22nd Manchesters attd. to 91st Brigade Signal Coy. and the case of Diptheria, Lieut J.C. Watson of the 2nd	

WAR DIARY
or
INTELLIGENCE SUMMARY.

Army Form C. 2118.

Place	Date	Hour	Summary of Events and Information	Remarks and references to Appendices
BERTRANCOURT	5/12/16		N.C.O's men of the 2nd Borders Regt were posted at MAILLY-MAILLET and the 2nd Queens, 218th Coy R.E. at P.18 carried. Gunners were inoculated with a view to finding a "carrier" whilst developed possible. Instruction of clothing & foundry work were continued.	
			T.S. Green Capt R.A.M.C.–T.	
			Production of the concentration of the Bienvoined area were continued. New latrine for BERTRANCOURT are being made. Water tests were being made of several sources of supply & water carts examined. N.C.O's men of the 2nd Gordons were posted at BERTRANCOURT. 126th Battery R.G.A. 95th Bty R.G.A., 9th Queens, 2nd Borders, & 22nd Bgde M.G. Coy at MAILLY-MAILLET. Instruction of clothing and foundry work were continued.	
			T.S. Green Capt R.A.M.C.–T.	

WAR DIARY or INTELLIGENCE SUMMARY.

Army Form C. 2118.

(Erase heading not required.)

Place	Date	Hour	Summary of Events and Information	Remarks and references to Appendices
BERTRANCOURT	6/12/16		I visited the laundry at AUTHIE and inspected the bath-houses at MAILLY-MAILLET and P.18 central. I also inspected part of the village of MAILLY-MAILLET. Routine inspections of the sanitary arrangements were continued in the Divisional area. Water testing was carried on & several water carts examined. N.C.O's & men of 9th Devons & 2nd Borders were bathed at MAILLY-MAILLET and the 24th Manchesters & 54th Coy R.E's at P.18 central. Disinfection of clothing & laundry work were continued. F. S. Carm. Capt R.A.M.C.-T.	
BERTRANCOURT	7/12/16		Routine sanitation inspections were continued in the Divisional area. The new fly proof latrines are being proceeded with in BERTRANCOURT. Water tests for the amount of chlorine to be added, were made at various supply posts & water carts examined.	

Place	Date	Hour	Summary of Events and Information	Remarks and references to Appendices

N.C.O's & men of the 2nd Gordons were bathed at BERTRANCOURT, 9th Devons at MAILLY-MAILLET and the 24th Manchesters & 54th Coy R. Co at P.18. central. Disinfection of clothing & laundry work were continued.

F. S. Carson. Capt. R.A.M.C.-T.

BERTRANCOURT.

8/12/16

I inspected the bath. houses at MAILLY-MAILLET and P.18. central and part of the village of MAILLY-MAILLET.

Routine inspections of the sanitary arrangements in the Divisional area were made.

Water testing & the inspection of water carts were continued.

N.C.Ob & men of the 8th Devons were bathed at BERTRANCOURT, 2nd Borders 1st South Staffords & 22nd Manchesters at MAILLY-MAILLET and the 24th Manchesters, 9th Devons & 20th Bgde Grenade Coy at P.18. central.

Laundry work & the Disinfection of clothing were carried on.

F. S. Carson Capt. R.A.M.C.-T.

WAR DIARY or INTELLIGENCE SUMMARY

Army Form C. 2118.

Place	Date	Hour	Summary of Events and Information	Remarks and references to Appendices
BERTRANCOURT	9/12/16		Routine inspections of the Divisional area were carried on by the inspectors of the Section. Water testing & the examination of water carts were continued. The case of suspected Diphtheria - N° 82695 Pte 6 Coy, 8th Devons was investigated & the billet disinfected. N.C.O's & men of the 8th Devons were bathed at BERTRANCOURT, and the 22nd Bgde Hqr troops, 24th Manchesters & 35th Batt R.G.A. at MAILLY-MAILLET. Laundry work & the disinfection of clothing were proceeded with. F. S. Carson. Capt R.A.M.C.-T.	
BERTRANCOURT	10/12/16		Inspections of the sanitary arrangements in the Divisional area were made. Water testing & the examination of water carts were continued. The billet occupied by Capt. Hart of the 23rd Field Ambulance a case of suspected Typhoid was disinfected. N.C.O's & men of the 2nd Border Regt, 7th Divl Signal Coy, 20th Brigade T.M.	

WAR DIARY
or
INTELLIGENCE SUMMARY

Army Form C. 2118.

Place	Date	Hour	Summary of Events and Information	Remarks and references to Appendices
BERTRANCOURT	11.2.16		In the morning J inspected the Divisional Bath Houses at BERTRANCOURT, MAILLY MAILLET, and MAILLY WOOD. Routine sanitary inspections were made in the area and the testing of water and examination of water carts continued. NCO's and men of the 1st R.W.F. were bathed at BERTRANCOURT, 91st Bde. HQ and 22nd Manchesters at MAILLY MAILLY and 8th Devons, Norcross and 12½ Corps North Lancs at MAILLY WOOD. Laundry work and the disinfection of clothing were continued.	T.S. Crum Capt R.A.M.C.

T.S. Crum Capt R.A.M.C.

WAR DIARY or INTELLIGENCE SUMMARY.

(Erase heading not required.)

Army Form C. 2118.

Place	Date	Hour	Summary of Events and Information	Remarks and references to Appendices
BERTRANCOURT	12-12-16		I took over command of the Sanitary Section this morning, Captain J S Carson the O.C. having gone on leave last night. Sanitary Inspections were continued in the Divisional area. A case of suspected Diphtheria in the 9th Devons was investigated and the necessary precautions were taken. N.C.O's and men of 2nd H.A.C, 20th Manchesters, 17th Northumberland Fusiliers, 21st Manchesters, 12th Loyal North Lancs, 8th Cavalry Pioneers and Divisional Engineers were bathed in the three bath houses. Laundry and disinfection work were continued. The area D.A.Q.M.G called with reference to proposed sanitary improvements in the area. Clean socks were issued to men in front line trenches. T Hardy. Lieut. RAMC	

WAR DIARY
or
INTELLIGENCE SUMMARY.

(Erase heading not required.)

Army Form C. 2118.

Instructions regarding War Diaries and Intelligence Summaries are contained in F. S. Regs., Part II. and the Staff Manual respectively. Title pages will be prepared in manuscript.

Place	Date	Hour	Summary of Events and Information	Remarks and references to Appendices
BERTRANCOURT	13.12.16		Routine sanitary inspections and inspections of water carts were continued in the area.	
			23959 Pte Watts, a case of suspected diphtheria in the 1st South Staffords was investigated and the billet was disinfected	
			Laundry work and disinfection of clothing were continued.	
			NCO's and men of 2nd HAC were bathed at BERTRANCOURT, 21st Manchesters at MAILLY MAILLET and 22nd Brigade HQ units, 1st R.Welsh Fusiliers + 2nd Warwicks at MAILLY WOOD.	
			Clean socks were provided for men in front line trenches and men on working parties	

T. Hardy, Lieut. RAMC.

2353   Wt. W2544/1454   700,000   5/15   D. D. & L.   A.D.S.S./Forms/C. 2118.

WAR DIARY or INTELLIGENCE SUMMARY.

Army Form C. 2118.

(Erase heading not required.)

Place	Date	Hour	Summary of Events and Information	Remarks and references to Appendices
BERTRANCOURT	14.12.16		Routine sanitary inspections were continued in the area. Water from various supplies was tested. Laundry work and disinfection were continued. Blankets from the 21st Field Ambulance were disinfected. N.C.Os and men of 2nd H.A.C. were bathed at BERTRANCOURT, 21st Manchesters and 91st M.G.C. at MAILLY MAILLET and 1st R. Welsh Fusiliers and 24th Manchesters at MAILLY WOOD. Clean socks were issued to 20th Inf. Brigade for men in the trenches. T. Moody Lieut. RAMC	
BERTRANCOURT	15.12.16		I visited the laundry at AUTHIE and made arrangements to increase the supply of clean socks. The sanitary inspection of the area was continued. Further water tests were made and the sources of supply marked as to the suitability for drinking purposes.	

WAR DIARY
or
INTELLIGENCE SUMMARY.
(Erase heading not required.)

Army Form C. 2118.

Instructions regarding War Diaries and Intelligence Summaries are contained in F. S. Regs., Part II. and the Staff Manual respectively. Title pages will be prepared in manuscript.

Place	Date	Hour	Summary of Events and Information	Remarks and references to Appendices
			NCOs and men of 2nd Warwicks were bathed at BERTRANCOURT, 91st Brigade H.Q. units at MAILLY MAILLET and 24th Manchesters, 22nd M.G.C and 2nd Warwick at MAILLY WOOD.	
			Clean socks were issued to two battalions of 20th Brigade and 91st Brigade Pioneers.	
			Laundry work and disinfection were continued. Blankets of Prisoners of War were disinfected	
			T. Sturdy, Lieut. RAMC	
BERTRANCOURT	16.12.16		I attended a conference of Sanitary Officers of XIII Corps at H.Q. D.M.S V Army. The conference was of a preliminary nature and was called to assist coordination in the new area.	
			The routine sanitary inspections were continued in the Divisional area.	

2353 Wt. W2544/1454 700,000 5/15 D. D. & L.   A.D.S.S./Forms/C. 2118.

WAR DIARY
or
INTELLIGENCE SUMMARY.
(Erase heading not required.)

Army Form C. 2118.

Instructions regarding War Diaries and Intelligence Summaries are contained in F. S. Regs., Part II. and the Staff Manual respectively. Title pages will be prepared in manuscript.

Place	Date	Hour	Summary of Events and Information	Remarks and references to Appendices
			The testing and labelling of water supplies was continued. Blankets from the 21st Field Ambulance were disinfected. NCOs and men of 20th Manchesters were bathed at BERTRANCOURT, 20th and 91st Brigade HQ troops at MAILLY MAILLET and 24th Manchesters at MAILLY WOOD. Clean socks for men in the trenches were issued to four battalions. Laundry work and disinfection were continued. T. Lloyd. Lieut RAMC	
BERTRANCOURT	17.12.16		In the afternoon I inspected the bath houses at MAILLY MAILLET and MAILLY WOOD to make arrangements for ironing the mens' service uniform while they were bathing. Routine Sanitary inspections were continued.	

Place	Date	Hour	Summary of Events and Information	Remarks and references to Appendices
			One case of DIPHTHERIA (2/Lieut J.A Spurling - 22nd Howitzer and 18267 L/cpl Jw Evans - 26th MGC) were investigated and the necessary precautions taken.	
			NCO's i/mcs of 29th Queen's were billeted at BERTRANCOURT, 26th MGC at MAILLY MAILLET and 26th Howitzers, 9/R Devons and 22nd Queen's at MAILLY WOOD.	
			Laundry work + disinfection of clothing were continued. Crown orders were issued to three battalions for noise in the trenches. 15 ord from PARIS	
BERTRANCOURT	18.7.16		In the morning I arranged our cooking room for the BERTRANCOURT Bath House. A hut was removed from a camp in the village and rebuilt so as to contain the bath house. Routine sanitary inspections were made in the area.	
			NCO's i/mcs of 21st Howitzers and 1st South Staffs were billeted at BERTRANCOURT, 9/R Devons	

WAR DIARY or INTELLIGENCE SUMMARY.

Army Form C. 2118.

(Erase heading not required.)

Place	Date	Hour	Summary of Events and Information	Remarks and references to Appendices
			at MAILLY MAILLET and MAILLY WOOD. Clean socks were issued to two battalions for men in the trenches. Laundry work and disinfection were continued. The blankets of 1st R Welsh Fusiliers were disinfected. T. Sloidy, Lieut. RAMC	
BERTRANCOURT	19.12.16		Routine inspections of billets etc. in the sanitary area were continued. N.C.O's and men of 8th Devons and 1st South Staffords were bathed at BERTRANCOURT, the 2nd Gordons at MAILLY MAILLET and 24th Manchesters and 8th Cavalry Pioneers at MAILLY WOOD. Laundry and disinfection work was continued. Blankets of 22nd Infantry Brigade were disinfected. Clean socks were issued to two battalions for men in the trenches. T. Sloidy, Lieut. RAMC	

Place	Date	Hour	Summary of Events and Information	Remarks and references to Appendices
BERTRANCOURT	30.7.16			

In the morning I went to MAILLY MAILLET to arrange for sanitary work to be done in the village. Also inspected the death house in the village.

Routine sanitary inspections were made in the area, in particular the area recently taken over by the division. Latrines at LOUVENCOURT and VAUCHELLES OR's were found clear, but the sanitary arrangements were once more the minor source of water supply in BERTRANCOURT were located and notices posted stating the purpose for which each was to be used.

NCO's and men of 1st South Staffords, 9th MGC, 21st and 22nd howitzers were bathed at BERTRANCOURT, 3rd Field Ambulance, 3rd Gordons & 1/3 Durham RE's at MAILLY MAILLET and 5th Notts & and 8th Cavalry Pioneers at MAILLY WOOD.

Clean socks were issued to those battalions for men in trenches.

Remarks work reinforcements of 22nd Inf. Brigade Headqrs were examined.

Blood, Lieut RAMC

Place	Date	Hour	Summary of Events and Information	Remarks and references to Appendices
BERTRANCOURT	21.12.16		Routine sanitary inspections were continued. Two cases of clinical DYSENTERY (27041 Pte. S. Barform, 2nd Borders and 40086 Pte. F. Johnson, 20th Manchesters) were investigated. The minor water supplies at MAILLY MAILLET were tested and the necessary notices posted. NCOs & men of Divisional units were bathed at BERTRANCOURT, 9th Devons and 2nd Borders at MAILLY MAILLET and 24th Manchesters and 2nd Gordons at MAILLY WOOD. Clean socks were issued to two battalions for men in the trenches. Laundry work & disinfection of clothing was continued. Blankets of 20th Manchesters and 2nd HAC were disinfected. T. Lloyd, Lieut R.A.M.C	

WAR DIARY
or
INTELLIGENCE SUMMARY.

(Erase heading not required.)

Army Form C. 2118.

Place	Date	Hour	Summary of Events and Information	Remarks and references to Appendices
BERTRANCOURT	22.12.16		In the morning lectures on the OC 3rd Divisional Ammunition Column of 3rd Divisional BAC's at BUS with reference to the possibility of 1st Divisional Corps getting at their posts at LOUVENCOURT. Routine sanitary inspection were continued in the battery area at VAUCHELLES. The minor work carried at BERTRANCOURT were that of the necessary no tree posts. Three cases of Scabies observed and three of suspected diptheria were investigated and the billets disinfected. NCO's men of 21st & 22nd Howitzers, 1st & 2nd Batteries and 2nd batteries were billeted at BERTRANCOURT, 20th Bde Ambulance and 20th MGC at MAILLY MAILLET and 22nd Bn Howitzers and 2nd Gordons at MAILLY HOOD. Clean baths were issued to four battalions in the twenty four hours and disinfectors of 22nd Brigade December.	T. Mark, Lieut ADMS

2353 Wt. W2544/1454 700,000 5/15 D.D.&L. AD.S.S/Forms/C. 2118.

WAR DIARY or INTELLIGENCE SUMMARY.

(Erase heading not required.)

Army Form C. 2118.

Place	Date	Hour	Summary of Events and Information	Remarks and references to Appendices
BERTRANCOURT	23-12-16		I visited the O.C. 3rd Divisional Baths again with reference to the use of their baths at LOUVENCOURT. I also saw the R.E. Officer i/c of water supply in Auchonvillers area and borrowed a plan of the supply. Sanitary inspections were continued at MAILLY MAILLET The testing of minor supplies of water at BERTRANCOURT was continued. N.C.O's and men of Divisional units were bathed at BERTRANCOURT, 2nd Borders and 22nd Manchesters at MAILLY MAILLET and 2nd Gordons and 24th Manchesters at MAILLY WOOD Clean socks were issued to two battalions for men in the trenches A case of MEASLES (140045 Gnr. G.W. Rogers) in 14 Brigade R.H.A. "T" Battery was investigated and the billet disinfected. Laundry work and disinfection of blankets and clothing were continued	

F. Flody Lieut. R.A.M.C.

WAR DIARY
or
INTELLIGENCE SUMMARY.

(Erase heading not required.)

Army Form C. 2118.

Instructions regarding War Diaries and Intelligence Summaries are contained in F. S. Regs., Part II. and the Staff Manual respectively. Title pages will be prepared in manuscript.

Place	Date	Hour	Summary of Events and Information	Remarks and references to Appendices
BERTRANCOURT	24.12.16		I resumed command of the Sanitary Section this morning. Sanitary Inspections and the testing of water supplies in the area were continued. N.C.O's and men of Divisional units were bathed at the BERTRANCOURT bath house, 8th Devons and 20th Brigade H.Q. units at MAILLY MAILLET and 21st and 24th Manchesters, 8th Devons and 2nd Gordons at MAILLY WOOD. Clean socks were issued to three battalions for men in the trenches. Laundry work and disinfection of clothing were continued. Blankets from No 37 Prisoners of War Company, were disinfected. _F. S. Carson. Capt. R.A.M.C_	
BERTRANCOURT	25.12.16		In the morning I visited several of the camps in and around BERTRANCOURT with a view to making schemes	

2353 Wt. W2544/1454 700,000 5/15 **D. D. & L.** A.D.S.S./Forms/C. 2118.

Place	Date	Hour	Summary of Events and Information	Remarks and references to Appendices
			for their sanitation and to decide upon sites for latrines, ablution benches etc, which the Engineers were to build. A case of Sus/Diphtheria (27193 Pte. A.J. Tales - 5th S.W.B.) and one of Sus/Cerebro Spinal Meningitis (81051 Spr. J. Campbell, 206 Coy. R.E.) were investigated and the billets disinfected. The Divisional Bath Houses were closed for the day. F. S. Carson Capt RAMC	
BERTRANCOURT	26.12.16		In the morning I was engaged on the preparation of schemes for the sanitation of hut camps in and about BERTRANCOURT. Plans were made of each camp and existing and proposed sites for sanitary conveniences marked. In the afternoon I inspected the Divisional Laundry at AUTHIE.	

WAR DIARY
or
INTELLIGENCE SUMMARY.
(Erase heading not required.)

Army Form C. 2118.

Instructions regarding War Diaries and Intelligence Summaries are contained in F. S. Regs., Part II. and the Staff Manual respectively. Title pages will be prepared in manuscript.

Place	Date	Hour	Summary of Events and Information	Remarks and references to Appendices
			Sanitary inspections were continued in the area.	
			NCOs and men of the 2nd Borders and 21st Field Ambce were bathed at MAILLY MAILLET and men of the Divisional Artillery at the 3rd Divisional Baths at LOUVENCOURT, which bath house we use, by arrangement, on Tuesdays and Wednesdays.	
			Clean socks were issued to four battalions for men in the trenches.	
			Laundry and disinfection work were continued	
			7. S. Carson. Capt RAMC	
BERTRANCOURT	27.12.16		I went to RAINCHEVAL to select a suitable place for a Bath House for the use of the Divisional Depôt. I also inspected this village as regards its sanitary condition and found the arrangements	

2353 Wt. W2544/1454 700,000 5/15 **D. D. & L.**   A.D.S.S./Forms/C. 2118.

WAR DIARY or INTELLIGENCE SUMMARY

satisfactory although the ventilation and lighting of some of the billets require improving.

Testing of water and the fixing of notices on the supplies were done at AUCHONVILLERS.

N.C.Os and men of the 20th Manchesters were bathed at BERTRANCOURT, 22nd Manchesters and 22nd T.M.B. at MAILLY MAILLET and 22nd M.G.C and 6th Cavalry Bde. Pioneers at MAILLY WOOD.

Clean socks were issued to three battalions for men in the trenches.

A case of German measles (12942 Pte. D. Graber - 2nd Queen's) and one of Susp. Para Typhoid (48292 Dvr. Loft - 7th D.A.C.) were investigated and the necessary precautions taken.

Laundry and Disinfection work were continued.

F. S. Carson. Capt. RAMC

WAR DIARY
or
INTELLIGENCE SUMMARY.

(Erase heading not required.)

Place	Date	Hour	Summary of Events and Information	Remarks and references to Appendices
BERTRANCOURT	25.12.16		I went to BEAUSSART to select a suitable place for a bath house. Owing to the lack of suitable units supply this was impossible. Sanitary inspections were made at BEAUSSART and MAILLY MAILLET. NCO's and men of the 1st R Welsh Fusiliers were billeted at BERTRANCOURT, 23rd Fusiliers, 8th Devon and 91st Bde Canade Coy at MAILLY MAILLET and 31st Honorlotte and Divisional Pioneers at MAILLY MCR. Green Cases were issued to two stations for men at the trencher. A case of Ins/Entero (27943 Pr. O. Pankhurst — 1st (?) R & 3rd Pnr. 3rd S&B) were investigated and the bullets and 21st steel andes and a case of Env/Gonde Special Maurafato demanded. Sanitary work over this batches was continuous.	

F. S. Cowan. Capt RAMC

WAR DIARY or INTELLIGENCE SUMMARY.

Army Form C. 2118.

(Erase heading not required.)

Place	Date	Hour	Summary of Events and Information	Remarks and references to Appendices
BERTRANCOURT	29.12.16		I went to LOUVENCOURT to make an inspection of the village as regards its sanitary condition.	

Sanitary inspections were made in the Divisional Artillery area at VAUCHELLES and LOUVENCOURT, and further work was done in connection with the sanitation of the BERTRANCOURT Camps.

One case of TYPHOID (33484 Pte A.J. Barnfield - 8th Devons) three cases of clinical dysentery and seven cases of sus/dysentery were investigated.

N.C.Os and men of the 1st Royal Welsh Fusiliers, and 2nd Warwicks were bathed at BERTRANCOURT, 1st South Staffords and 95th Coy. R.E.'s at MAILLY MAILLET and 21st Manchesters and Pioneer Battalion at MAILLY WOOD.

Clean sock were issued to five battalions for men in the trenches.

Laundry and disinfection work were continued

F. S. Carson. Capt RAMC

WAR DIARY
or
INTELLIGENCE SUMMARY

Army Form C. 2118.

Place	Date	Hour	Summary of Events and Information	Remarks and references to Appendices
BERTRANCOURT	30.12.16		In the morning General an inspection of the billets at VAUCHELLES as regards its sanitary condition. Routine sanitary inspections were made in the Divisional area. Water fatigues were carried out at VAUCHELLES.	
			NCO's and men of 9th Warwicks, 3rd H.L.I. and Divisional Train were billeted at BERTRANCOURT, 1st South Staffords, Batt. H.Q. and 20th & 23rd E's at Mailly Maillet and 2nd Queens, 24th Manchester and 6th Cameron Pioneers at MAILLY WOOD.	
			Orders were issued to these battalions for men in the trenches.	
			A case of Chinese Desertion (9753 4/39 Labourer - 9th Warwicks) was investigated. Rumours work and arrangements of capture are continued.	
			T. S. Edwin. Capt. BMV.T	

WAR DIARY or INTELLIGENCE SUMMARY

Army Form C. 2118.

Place	Date	Hour	Summary of Events and Information	Remarks and references to Appendices
BERTRANCOURT	31.12.16		Routine sanitary inspections were made in the Divisional area. Inspections of water carts were continued. NCO's and men of 2nd H.A.C. and 2nd Warwicks were bathed at BERTRANCOURT, 1st South Staffords, 9th Devons and Divisional Engineers at MAILLY MAILLET and 24th Manchester, 91st T.M.B. and 6th Cavalry Pioneers at MAILLY WOOD. Clean socks were issued to five battalions for men in the trenches. Laundry work and disinfection were continued. F. S. Carson. Capt. R.A.M.C.T.	

N⁰ 10 SECTION.
2ᴺᴰ LONDON SANITARY COY: R.A.M.C.T.

B.E.F. FRANCE.

7ᵗʰ D.⟩.

CONFIDENTIAL.

140/94/

Vol 6

Jan. 1917

~ WAR DIARY ~

—— 1ˢᵗ JANUARY 1917 ~ 31ˢᵗ JANUARY 1917 ——

— VOL: 6 ~

COMMITTEE FOR THE
MEDICAL HISTORY OF THE WAR

Date   13 MAR. 1917

WAR DIARY or INTELLIGENCE SUMMARY.

Army Form C. 2118.

(Erase heading not required.)

Place	Date	Hour	Summary of Events and Information	Remarks and references to Appendices
BERTRANCOURT	1.1.17		I inspected the Kaffir Camp at BERTRANCOURT and found the sanitary condition satisfactory. Routine Inspections were made in the area and the testing of water supplies was continued. A case of Typhoid Fever, one of suspected Diphtheria and one of suspected Dysentery were investigated and the necessary precautions were taken. NCOs & men of the 2nd HAC and 2nd Warwicks were bathed at BERTRANCOURT, 1st South Staffords, 9th Devons & Divisional Engineers at MAILLY MAILLET and 24th Manchesters, 91st Brigade TMB and 6th Cavalry Brigade Pioneers at MAILLY WOOD. Clean socks were issued to five battalions for men in trenches. Laundry work and the disinfection of blankets & clothing were carried out at FUTHIE. F.S. Carson Capt. RAMC	

WAR DIARY
—or—
INTELLIGENCE SUMMARY.

(Erase heading not required.)

Instructions regarding War Diaries and Intelligence Summaries are contained in F. S. Regs., Part II. and the Staff Manual respectively. Title pages will be prepared in manuscript.

Army Form C. 2118.

Place	Date	Hour	Summary of Events and Information	Remarks and references to Appendices
BERTRANCOURT	21.17		I visited the A.D.M.S. 7th Division with reference to the water supply of BEAUSSART, as the public wells in that village gave a very unsatisfactory water. I had conspicuous notice boards fixed on the two main wells in one case forbidding the use of the water to troops and the other stating that it was to be used for cooking only. Sanitary Inspections of the 91st Brigade Transport lines were made. One case of Clinical Dysentery was investigated and the necessary sanitary precautions taken. NCOs & men of 22nd Manchesters and 65th Siege Battery were bathed at Mailly Maillet, 7th Divisional Details at BERTRANCOURT and 24th Manchesters & 22nd Bde. Clearing party at MAILLY WOOD. Clean socks for men in trenches were issued to three battalions. Blankets of the 2nd Gordons were disinfected. Laundry work was continued.	

2353 Wt. W2544/1454 700,000 5/15 **D. D. & L.**   A.D.S.S./Forms/C. 2118.

F. S. Cairns Capt. RAMC

WAR DIARY or INTELLIGENCE SUMMARY.

(Erase heading not required.)

Army Form C. 2118.

Place	Date	Hour	Summary of Events and Information	Remarks and references to Appendices
BERTRANCOURT	3/1/17		I went to AUCHONVILLERS, the SUCRERIE and MAILLY MAILLET to inspect and trace the water supplies of the forward area.	

I inspected sixteen water carts which were refilling at the MAILLY MAILLET supply and found that in many cases there was no man trained in water duties on the cart and that chlorination of water in some cases was not properly carried out.

Sanitary inspections of the 91st M.G.C. and T.M.B. at MAILLY MAILLET and the 5th South Wales Borderers at AUCHONVILLERS were made by the Inspectors of the Section.

Five cases of suspected Dysentery and three cases of Clinical Dysentery were investigated and sanitary precautions taken.

NCOs & men of the 2nd Warwicks and 22nd M.G.C. were bathed at BERTRANCOURT, 22nd Manchesters, 20th MGC & 22nd Grenade Coy at MAILLY MAILLET and 24th Manchesters, 5th South Wales Borderers & 6th Cavalry Pioneers at MAILLY WOOD.

Blankets of the 20th M.G.C. were disinfected

Place	Date	Hour	Summary of Events and Information	Remarks and references to Appendices
BERTRANCOURT	4.1.17			

laundry work and the disinfector of clothing were continued. Green cards were issued to the 3rd Division for men in the trenches.

F.S. Eason. Capt. R.A.M.C

I went to BUS to inspect the water supplies of the village and found them satisfactory. I inspected a number of wells and water which were retaining at the standpipes and again found that in many cases there were no new or the suspected cases of enteric dysentery were investigated and the necessary sanitary precautions taken.

N.C.O.'s & men of the 4th Divisional Train and 1st R.M3 were billeted at BERTRANCOURT, 3rd Howitzers, 91st & 23rd Siege Coys and 9th? Field Ambce at MAILLY MAILLET and 5th SWB and 21st Howitzers at MAILLY WOOD.

Place	Date	Hour	Summary of Events and Information	Remarks and references to Appendices
			Clean socks were issued to two battalions for men in trenches. Disinfection of clothing and laundry work were continued. The blankets of 20th T.M.B. were disinfected. F. S. Carson. Capt. RAMC	
BERTRANCOURT	5.1.17		I visited the 7th Divisional Laundry at AUTHIE to make further arrangements for the supply of clean clothing. Routine sanitary inspections were made in the area + the testing of water supplies was continued. NCOs & men of the 7th Divisional Train and Details were bathed at BERTRANCOURT, 2nd Borders and 91st M.G.C. at MAILLY MAILLET and 24th Manchesters and 5th SWB at MAILLY WOOD. Clean socks were issued to two battalions for men in trenches. Laundry work and the disinfection of clothing and blankets were continued. F. S. Carson. Capt. RAMC	

WAR DIARY

or

INTELLIGENCE SUMMARY.

(Erase heading not required.)

Army Form C. 2118.

Instructions regarding War Diaries and Intelligence Summaries are contained in F. S. Regs., Part II. and the Staff Manual respectively. Title pages will be prepared in manuscript.

Place	Date	Hour	Summary of Events and Information	Remarks and references to Appendices
BERTRANCOURT	6·1·17		I made an inspection of the village of BERTRANCOURT and the camps in the vicinity of the village. I found the sanitary conditions satisfactory although in some cases inadequate. The work of providing additional accommodation was progressing.	
			Routine sanitary inspections were carried out in the area. A number of water carts were examined. as also were the water storage tanks at the Brewery water supply MAILLY MAILLET.	
			N.C.O.s + men of 4th Durm Train and 9th Devons were bathed at BERTRANCOURT, 54th and 95th Companies RE. + 2nd Borders at MAILLEY MAILLET and 5th SWB + 24th Manchesters at MAILLY WOOD	
			Clean socks were issued to two battalions for men in trenches. Laundry and disinfection work were continued. Blankets of the Divisional Rest Station ACHEUX and from 7th Durm Depôt were disinfected.	
			F. S. Carson, Capt. RAMC	

2353 Wt. W2544/1454 700,000 5/15 **D. D. & L.** A.D.S.S./Forms/C. 2118.

WAR DIARY or INTELLIGENCE SUMMARY.

(Erase heading not required.)

Army Form C. 2118.

Place	Date	Hour	Summary of Events and Information	Remarks and references to Appendices
BERTRANCOURT	7.1.17		In the morning I went to LOUVENCOURT to arrange for the use of the Bath House by the 7th Division. In the afternoon I went to 7th Divisional Headquarters to make arrangements for handing over the baths and laundry arrangements of the Division. The 17th Northumberland Fusiliers were inspected at MAILLY MAILLET and routine Sanitary inspections were continued. One case of suspected Diphtheria was investigated and the billet disinfected. NCO's and men of the 7th Divisional Train and Details were bathed at BERTRANCOURT, 2nd Borders & 21st + 22nd Field Ambulance at MAILLY MAILLET, and 5th S.W.B. and details at MAILLY WOOD. Clean socks were issued to five battalions for men in the trenches. Laundry work was continued and blankets from the 22nd Field Ambulance were disinfected. F. S. Carson. Capt RAMC	

WAR DIARY
or
INTELLIGENCE SUMMARY.

(Erase heading not required.)

Army Form C. 2118.

Instructions regarding War Diaries and Intelligence Summaries are contained in F. S. Regs., Part II. and the Staff Manual respectively. Title pages will be prepared in manuscript.

Place	Date	Hour	Summary of Events and Information	Remarks and references to Appendices
BERTRANCOURT	8.1.17		I went to AUTHIE to make arrangements for the disposal and treatment of the waste water from the laundry. A scheme was drawn up to adapt some existing tanks for the treatment.	
			One case of Dysentery, one of measles + one of suspected Diphtheria were investigated + the billets disinfected	
			NCO's + men of the 9th Devons were bathed at BERTRANCOURT 2nd Queens and 20th + 1/3 Durham R.E.'s at MAILLY MAILLET and the 21st Manchesters + 20th M.G.C at MAILLY WOOD	
			Clean socks for men in the trenches were issued to these battalions	
			Sanitary Inspections were made in the forward area.	
			Laundry work + the disinfection of clothing were continued	
			F.S. Carson, Capt. RAMC	
BERTRANCOURT	9.1.17		I examined and questioned a number of men of the	

2353 Wt. W2544/1454 700,000 5/15 D. D. & L. A.D.S.S./Forms/C. 2118.

WAR DIARY or INTELLIGENCE SUMMARY.

(Erase heading not required.)

Army Form C. 2118.

Place	Date	Hour	Summary of Events and Information	Remarks and references to Appendices
			2nd Gordons endeavouring to trace a 'carrier' or 'carriers' of Diphtheria. Three men were noted as suspected 'carriers' and reported to the A.D.M.S. Two cases of suspected diphtheria and one case of clinical Dysentery were investigated and the billets disinfected. Routine sanitary inspections were made in the area. NCOs & men of the 2nd Gordons were bathed at BERTRANCOURT, 2nd Queens and 1/3 Durham R.E. at MAILLY MAILLET and the 5th SWB and 24th Manchesters at MAILLY WOOD. Clean socks for men in the trenches were issued to two battalions. Blankets from the 7th Divisional School and Divl. Depot were disinfected. Laundry work was continued. F. S. Carson Capt. RAMC.	
BERTRANCOURT	10.1.17		In the morning I inspected several Cafés in BERTRANCOURT	

WAR DIARY
or
INTELLIGENCE SUMMARY.

(Erase heading not required.)

Army Form C. 2118.

Instructions regarding War Diaries and Intelligence Summaries are contained in F. S. Regs., Part II. and the Staff Manual respectively. Title pages will be prepared in manuscript.

Place	Date	Hour	Summary of Events and Information	Remarks and references to Appendices
			who were selling coffee & other drinks to troops, made from water not obtained from approved sources. These were reported to the Town Commandant for further action.	
			In the afternoon I visited the Laundry at HUTHIE.	
			The testing of the main water supplies in the area was continued	
			NCOs & men of the 2nd Gordons and 22nd Manchesters were bathed at BERTRANCOURT, 2nd Queens at MAILLY MAILLET and 24th Manchesters and 2nd Queens at MAILLY WOOD	
			Socks for men in the trenches were issued to three battalions.	
			Laundry and Disinfection work were continued	
			J.J. Carson, Capt. RAMCT	
BERTRANCOURT	11.1.17		A Sanitary Inspection of the RAILHEAD AT BEAUSSART	

2353 Wt. W2544/1454 700,000 5/15 D. D. & L. A.D.S.S./Forms/C. 2118.

Place	Date	Hour	Summary of Events and Information	Remarks and references to Appendices
			shewed that the sanitation was unsatisfactory. The water supplies at MAILLY MAILLET were again tested and found satisfactory. Laundry work & disinfection of clothing were continued. NCOs & men of 2nd Gordons, 22nd Manchesters and 7th Divisional Train were bathed at BERTRANCOURT, 2nd HAC and 7th D.A.C. at MAILLY MAILLET and 20th, 24th Manchesters at MAILLY WOOD. Further work was done at the Laundry at AUTHIE on the scheme for treatment of waste water. F.J. Carson, Capt. RAMC	
BERTRANCOURT	12/1/17		I took swabs of the three suspected Diphtheria carriers in the 2nd Gordons and sent them to the Mobile Laboratory. In the afternoon I visited the Laundry at AUTHIE.	

Place	Date	Hour	Summary of Events and Information	Remarks and references to Appendices
BERTRANCOURT	13.1.17		I went to BERUSSART RAILHEAD and made a careful inspection. Found it in a very unsanitary condition. A return was drawn up to improve its existing conditions. In the evening, I attended a meeting of Sanitary Officers at I Corps Headquarters. Routine sanitary inspections were made in of area and	

7-S Essen Corps REMCI

continued.

In the battalion laundry work the disinfection of clothing was

NCOs and men of 2/4 Gordons & 9th Devons were bathed at BERTRANCOURT, 2/2 H.A.C at MAILLY MAILLET and the 2½ Hampshires and 3/ Warwicks at MAILLY WOOD.

Clean socks were issued for men in the Trenches

and several urine tests were examined.

The testing of water supplies in the area was continued.

WAR DIARY or INTELLIGENCE SUMMARY.

Army Form C. 2118.

(Erase heading not required.)

Place	Date	Hour	Summary of Events and Information	Remarks and references to Appendices
			a number of water carts were examined when refilling at the MAILLY-MAILLET supply.	
			Two cases of Measles were investigated and the billets disinfected. A suspected case of Meningitis was reported among the civil population at BERTRANCOURT. On investigation this was proved to be Broncho-Pulmonary Meningitis.	
			NCOs & men of the 2nd Gordons & 22nd M.G.C. were bathed at BERTRANCOURT, 168th Battery R.F.A., 91st Bde. Grenade Coy & 7th Divn. Salvage Coy, at MAILLY MAILLET and 2nd Warwicks and 20th Manchesters at MAILLY WOOD. Laundry work and the disinfection of clothing were continued.	
			F. S. Carson Capt. R.A.M.C.	
BERTRANCOURT	14.1.17		NCOs & men of the 2nd Queens and 7th Divn. Signals were bathed at BERTRANCOURT, 20th M.G.C., 14th Bde. R.H.A. and 161st, 155 Bty. R.F.A. at MAILLY MAILLET and 1st S.Staffords & 24th Manchesters at MAILLY WOOD. Clean socks were issued to the 1st S.Staffords and 2nd Warwicks for	

WAR DIARY
or
INTELLIGENCE SUMMARY.

(Erase heading not required.)

Army Form C. 2118.

Instructions regarding War Diaries and Intelligence Summaries are contained in F. S. Regs., Part II. and the Staff Manual respectively. Title pages will be prepared in manuscript.

Place	Date	Hour	Summary of Events and Information	Remarks and references to Appendices
			men in the trenches.	
			Civilian farmers in BERTRANCOURT were notified to remove accumulations of manure from their farm yards as in many case a foul effluent was running into the street.	
			Laundry work and disinfection of Clothing were continued Blankets from the 22nd field Ambulance were disinfected.	
			F.S. Caison, Capt. RAMC.	
BERTRANCOURT	15.1.17		I went to MAILLY MAILLET and inspected the water supplies of the forward area. I also inspected the bath houses at MAILLY MAILLET and MAILLY WOOD also the camps in MAILLY WOOD. The Sanitation of these camps was found satisfactory.	
			Other sanitary inspections were made in the area.	
			NCO's and men of the 20th M.GC were bathed at BERTRANCOURT, 22nd Manchesters + 35th Battery RHA at MAILLY MAILLET,	

2353   Wt. W2544/1454 700,000 5/15 D. D. & L.   A.D.S.S./Forms/C. 2118.

WAR DIARY
or
INTELLIGENCE SUMMARY.
(Erase heading not required.)

Army Form C. 2118.

Place	Date	Hour	Summary of Events and Information	Remarks and references to Appendices
			and the 21st Manchesters at MAILLY WOOD. Clean socks were issued to three battalions for men in the trenches. Laundry and disinfection routine work were continued. F.J. Carson. Cpl. RAMC	
BERTRANCOURT	16.1.17		I met the D.M.S. V Army by appointment at VAUCHELLES to make a sanitary inspection of the Divisional Schools in the village. Routine sanitary inspections were continued in the area and the testing of water supplies and fixing the necessary notices. NCO's and men of the 2nd H.A.C. and 2nd Warwicks were bathed at BERTRANCOURT, 20th Manchesters, 22nd M.G.C. and 13th Durham R.E. at MAILLY MAILLET and 24th Manchesters at MAILLY WOOD	

Place	Date	Hour	Summary of Events and Information	Remarks and references to Appendices
			Clean socks were issued to fine battalions for men in the trenches. Laundry work and the disinfection of clothing was continuous.	
			J.T. Cannan Col. R.A.M.C.	
BERGENCOURT	4.1.17		A scheme for the efficient sanitation of the villages at Moulin, Heulat was formulated and forwarded to the Senior Comm: 2nd Arm. It included for the erection of public latrines, tuck incinerators and refuse pouches. The following cases of infectious diseases were reported:- investigated :- One Cerebro Spinal Meningitis. One Measles. One Erysipelas. Diphtheria and Scarlet fever Dysentery. No necessary sanitary precautions were taken. A map was made of the water supplies of the farming area to facilitate further investigation. NCO's and men of 2/3 H.A.C. and 3rd Brigades were notified of	

WAR DIARY or INTELLIGENCE SUMMARY.

Army Form C. 2118.

(Erase heading not required.)

Place	Date	Hour	Summary of Events and Information	Remarks and references to Appendices
			BERTRANCOURT, 20th Manchesters and 2nd Queens at MAILLY MAILLET, 24th Manchester at MAILLY WOOD and 1st R.W.F. and Divisional Artillery at LOUVENCOURT. Clean socks for men in the trenches were issued to five battalions. Laundry work was continued. F.J. Causon Capt. RAMC	
BERTRANCOURT	18.1.17		I inspected the rations Refilling Points of the 4th Division at the time of issuing rations, and found that the methods in use made it practically impossible for food to be filled into the carts without getting soiled. This I reported together with suggestions for improvement. A scheme for the efficient sanitation of VAUCHELLES was prepared and sent together with a sketch plan of the village to the Town Commandant. Special sanitary arrangements were made at KAFFIR CAMP	

Place	Date	Hour	Summary of Events and Information	Remarks and references to Appendices
BERTRANCOURT	19.1.17		In the Nature Soulh Officers who were absent, came to the camp. Special instructions were given on the running of fires and examination of rations. One case of suspected Dysentery was reported & immediately NCOs train of 4 to 29 HLI and 2nd Tunnelers were posted at BERTRANCOURT. 1st Queens, 9th MGC + 233 Bde RGA at MAILLY MAILLET. 24th Punchahos at NIEULLY WOOD and 1st RWF and 7th DSC at LOUVENCOURT. The issue of clean socks to men in the trenches was continued. Laundry work since the destruction of clothing (blankets) are continued. A.T. Eaven Capt RAMC. In the morning I visited the hommeau at FLUTTE. A scheme was proposed for the treatment of scab with from the Divisional School Bath house at VAUCHELLES, and forwarded to the Medical Officer.	

WAR DIARY or INTELLIGENCE SUMMARY.

Army Form C. 2118.

Instructions regarding War Diaries and Intelligence Summaries are contained in F. S. Regs., Part II. and the Staff Manual respectively. Title pages will be prepared in manuscript.

(Erase heading not required.)

Place	Date	Hour	Summary of Events and Information	Remarks and references to Appendices
BERTRANCOURT	20.1.17		Two Cases of Suspected Dysentery were reported and investigated. NCOs & men of the 2nd H.A.C were bathed at BERTRANCOURT, 91st M.G.C and 233 Bty R.G.A at MAILLY MAILLET, 21st & 24th Manchesters at MAILLY WOOD and 1st R.W.F at LOUVENCOURT. The issue of clean socks for men in the trenches was continued. Laundry work & the disinfection of blankets and clothing were continued. F.J. Carson, Capt. RAMC In the morning I went to BEAUSSART and laid before the Town Commandant a scheme for the efficient sanitation of his village. It included for the erection of new public latrines, incinerators and ablution benches. I sent a NCO and man to VAUCHELLES to fix up a	

WAR DIARY
or
INTELLIGENCE SUMMARY.
(Erase heading not required.)

Army Form C. 2118.

Place	Date	Hour	Summary of Events and Information	Remarks and references to Appendices
PERRONCOURT	31.1.17		Public lectures and interests on matters to the town commencement. Sanitary inspection was continued in To area + hots were opened to various services of work at 4.15 pm. One issue of inspected Diphtheria and one of Rubeola Diphtheriaceu were reported and investigated. The letters were disinfected. NCOs men of 32nd M.G.C. and 31st Div ambulance were bathed at Mailly Maillet, and 26th Notts +Derby + 34th Trench mortars at MAILLY WOOD. Foundry work was continued. T. S. Coram Capt RAMC. In the morning I made a sanitary inspection of the villages of ACHEUX on instruction from No D.D.M.S. I corps. I found the sanitary arrangements were satisfactory.	

WAR DIARY or INTELLIGENCE SUMMARY.

Army Form C. 2118.

(Erase heading not required.)

Place	Date	Hour	Summary of Events and Information	Remarks and references to Appendices
			handed over the bath houses, as the 4th Division was moving to a rest area and the Sanitary Section was remaining behind. 4th Divisional Headquarters provided two motor lorries, and removed the clothing & equipment from the Divisional Bath houses to the Laundry at HUTHIE. The bath houses were closed down. NCO's of the Sanitary Section in charge of bath houses returned to the Sanitary Section. F.J. Carson, Capt. RAMC	
BERTRANCOURT	22.1.17		I met the D.D.M.S. I Corps by appointment at KEFIR CAMP, BERTRANCOURT and made a sanitary inspection with him. NCO's of the Sanitary Section were sent to VAUCHELLES, MAILLY MAILLET, MAILLY WOOD, BEAUSSART & BERTRANCOURT and attached to the respective Town Commandants as representatives of the	

Place	Date	Hour	Summary of Events and Information	Remarks and references to Appendices
PETERSDORP	23/11		Sunday service in the village, it subject was obedient on sanitary matters. Sources of water supply were fixed and notices fixed on various. Men conspicuous parade was put on a number of weeks.	

J.S. Carson, Capt. R.A.M.C.

I made a sanitary inspection at VAUCELLES and of the Divisional School in the vicinity of the village. I found that no progress had been made in the sanitation.

Sanitary inspections were continued over various of the returned units were inspected:- 4th Divisional ammunition Column, 135 Company R.E., No 1 camp Heavy Mortar Corps and 31st Howitzers.

Source water took were carried out.

for J.S. Carson Capt. R.A.M.C.

WAR DIARY
or
INTELLIGENCE SUMMARY.
(Erase heading not required.)

Army Form C. 2118.

WAR DIARY or INTELLIGENCE SUMMARY.

(Erase heading not required.)

Army Form C. 2118.

Place	Date	Hour	Summary of Events and Information	Remarks and references to Appendices
BERTRANCOURT	24.1.17		I inspected the various camps in the vicinity of BERTRANCOURT and found that progress was very slow as regards the fitting up of additional sanitary conveniences. I also inspected a number of small units on the BERTRANCOURT - HEDAUX Road. No. 2 Camp MAILLY MAILLET was inspected and found generally satisfactory. Water supplies of the villages of VAUCHELLES were tested and found to be still satisfactory. F.J. Carson, Capt. RAMC.	
BERTRANCOURT	25.1.17		I went to the AUTHIE, BEAUQUESNES & BEAUVAL area to conclude the handing over of the 7th Divisional Baths & Laundry and to give assistance in the starting of the baths in the rest area.	

Place	Date	Hour	Summary of Events and Information	Remarks and references to Appendices
BERTRANCOURT	26.11		Further improvements were made in the Camp. Reports from the various cookers in the camp showed that they had been little progress made. Minor water supplies of VITCHELLES were tested. B.J. Green Capt RAMC Inspected the WHITE CITY, BEAUMONT HAMEL and AUCHONVILLERS with reference to their sanitary condition, and water supply. I found that the sanitation at WHITE CITY and BEAUMONT HAMEL were neglected and required immediate attention. The sanitation of AUCHONVILLERS was good. Found that the water supply for the forward area was very unsatisfactory. Sandy Lane is chiefly used in a dirty condition and is of use. Further sanitary measures of tracks are more	

WAR DIARY or INTELLIGENCE SUMMARY.

Army Form C. 2118.

(Erase heading not required.)

Place	Date	Hour	Summary of Events and Information	Remarks and references to Appendices
			carried out in the area as also was the inspection of water carts. F.J. Causon Capt. RAMC	
BERTRANCOURT	27.1.17		I attended at 5th Corps Headquarters in the morning to see the D.D.M.S. by appointment with reference to the general sanitation of my area. I inspected "X" Camp BERTRANCOURT. Routine sanitary inspections of billets were made in the area. Water supplies of BERTRANCOURT were again tested and found to be satisfactory. F.J. Causon Capt. RAMC	
BERTRANCOURT	28.1.17		Routine sanitary inspections were made, the following units being inspected: 5th Corps Caterpillar Park, ASC, 208th Coy. R.E., 311th Brigade R.F.A., 47th Reserve Park ASC, and S Battery, R.H.A. These	

WAR DIARY
or
INTELLIGENCE SUMMARY.

(Erase heading not required.)

Army Form C. 2118.

Place	Date	Hour	Summary of Events and Information	Remarks and references to Appendices
BERTRANCOURT	29.11.17		units were situated in FICHEUX WOOD & MAILLY WOOD. Baths supplies at MAILLY MAILLET were again looked and found satisfactory.	
			J.S. Cowan Capt RAMC	
			In the afternoon I inspected the Harmony at FLIXIB. Sanitary improvements were made of the following works:-	
			3 H.P. Incinerators and 20ft Latts, + Dining Refectories. The question of the disposal of accumulation of manure at MAILLY MAILLET received attention and a list of such accumulations was handed to the Senior Commander for necessary action. The boiling of water and examination of water carts was continued. Cases at Deptilaria were inspected in the 50th Battn. RAMC Mo Nicol, a dugout near AUCHONVILLERS was disinfected.	
			J.S. Cowan Capt RAMC	

WAR DIARY or INTELLIGENCE SUMMARY.

Army Form C. 2118.

(Erase heading not required.)

Place	Date	Hour	Summary of Events and Information	Remarks and references to Appendices
BERTRANCOURT	30.1.17		I inspected the village of BEAUSSART and the RAILHEAD at BEAUSSART in the morning, and found that the sanitation was improving and that the work of erecting additional latrines &c. was progressing favourably. Other sanitary inspections made in the area were 22nd Divisional Train ASC and 19th Battery RGA. A case of Measles was reported in the 206th Field Company RE. The billet at No.2 Camp MAILLY WOOD was disinfected. The water from a new boring on the BERTRANCOURT - ACHEUX Road was tested and found satisfactory. It required one scoop of bleaching powder per water cart. F.S. Carson. Capt. RAMC.	
BERTRANCOURT	31.1.17		I inspected the village of MAILLY MAILLET and the Camps at MAILLY WOOD. At MAILLY MAILLET I found no progress	

WAR DIARY
or
INTELLIGENCE SUMMARY.

(*Erase heading not required.*)

Army Form C. 2118.

Instructions regarding War Diaries and Intelligence Summaries are contained in F. S. Regs., Part II. and the Staff Manual respectively. Title pages will be prepared in manuscript.

Place	Date	Hour	Summary of Events and Information	Remarks and references to Appendices
			in the erection of new sanitary conveniences. There was also a large amount of billet refuse and horse manure in the village. MAILLY WOOD was satisfactory	
			Routine sanitary inspections were made in the area. The testing of water supplies and examination of water carts were continued.	
			In the evening I attended a conference of Sanitary Officers at 5th Corps Headquarters, ACHEUX.	
			F.J. Carson, Capt. RAMC	

2353   Wt. W2544/1454   700,000   5/15   D. D. & L.   A.D.S.S./Forms/C. 2118.

WAR DIARY
or
INTELLIGENCE SUMMARY.

(Erase heading not required.)

Army Form C. 2118.

Instructions regarding War Diaries and Intelligence Summaries are contained in F. S. Regs., Part II. and the Staff Manual respectively. Title pages will be prepared in manuscript.

Place	Date	Hour	Summary of Events and Information	Remarks and references to Appendices

No. 10
SANITARY SECTION.

DDMS
II Corps

Herewith the "War Diary" of
the Section for the month of February.

F. S. Carson, Capt RAMC
O.C. 10 Sanitary Section

No 10 Section 10
2nd London Sanitary Coy. R.A.M.C.T.
B.E.F. France.

140/994

Confidential.

4th Division

Vol 7

Feb. 1917

- WAR DIARY -

from 1st Feb: to 28th Feb: 1917

Volume 7 -

COMMITTEE FOR THE
MEDICAL HISTORY OF THE WAR

Date   4 - APR. 1917

Place	Date	Hour	Summary of Events and Information	Remarks and references to Appendices
BERTRANCOURT	1.2.17		In the morning Swept to FETEUX WOOD and inspected huts in the hut camps as regards their Sanitation. Routine Sanitary inspections were made in the villages and camps in the area. Drafts two weeks Cotte were reexamined at MAILLY MAILLET as regards cleanliness and efficiency of chlorination. In nine cases it was found that the water was not Efficiently chlorinated. The testing of water supplies in the area and fixing up and setting the necessary notices were continued. 4.5. German Cap armlet.	
BERTRANCOURT	2.2.17		Swept to VAUCHELLES and made a sanitary inspection of the village and of the Divisional Salvage in the outskirts of the village. Issue the M.O. of the Divisional Salvage with reference to a scheme for the disposal of waste water from the Post House, and explained	

WAR DIARY
or
INTELLIGENCE SUMMARY.
(Erase heading not required.)

Army Form C. 2118.

Place	Date	Hour	Summary of Events and Information	Remarks and references to Appendices
			the details of the scheme to the R.E. Officer who had the work in hand. Routine sanitary inspections were made in the area including the Railhead at BELLE ÉGLISE. General water duties and testing of water supply was continued. At BEAUSSART progress was made in removing the accumulation of manure and refuse. Two men were obtained for permanent sanitary work at the BEAUSSART RAILHEAD. F. S. Carson, CAPT RAMC	
BERTRANCOURT	3.2.17		I inspected the camps "X" and "Y" at BERTRANCOURT and found the general sanitary condition unsatisfactory. I reported this condition to the A.D.M.S. 32nd Division and the Town Commandant. I sent the scheme of sanitation for the RAILHEAD	

Place	Date	Hour	Summary of Events and Information	Remarks and references to Appendices
BERGSSART			to the Officer % of the construction unit. This scheme included for special arrangements as regards latrines over the remainder of faces." As Native South Africans working parties the 5th Corps Area Officer called to see me this afternoon with reference to the distribution of m.o. personnel at the area. Routine sanitary inspections were continued at the area.
4.2 Garson Capt Remot	
BERINGSORT	14.9.17		Inspected the Railhead at BELLE EGLISE and found the sanitary condition generally satisfactory although there was insufficient latrine accommodation. I submitted a scheme for the improvement of sanitary arrangements. Medicine was destroyed for a report on well supplies at the area.	

WAR DIARY
or
INTELLIGENCE SUMMARY.
(Erase heading not required.)

Army Form C. 2118.

Instructions regarding War Diaries and Intelligence Summaries are contained in F. S. Regs., Part II. and the Staff Manual respectively. Title pages will be prepared in manuscript.

Place	Date	Hour	Summary of Events and Information	Remarks and references to Appendices
BERTRANCOURT	5.2.17		Routine sanitary inspections were carried out in the area. F. S. Carson, Capt. RAMC. I met the D.D.M.S. 5th Corps by appointment at BERTRANCOURT and made inspections with him in the village and in the camps in vicinity of the village. Progress was reported in the erection of sanitary conveniences at MAILLY MAILLET and camps in MAILLY WOOD were reported satisfactory. Schemes for the clarification of water from Bath Houses were sent to the Town Commandants. This work was held up by the frost. Routine sanitary inspections were carried out in the area. F. S. Carson, Capt. RAMC.	

WAR DIARY
or
INTELLIGENCE SUMMARY.

(Erase heading not required.)

Army Form C. 2118.

Instructions regarding War Diaries and Intelligence Summaries are contained in F. S. Regs., Part II. and the Staff Manual respectively. Title pages will be prepared in manuscript.

Place	Date	Hour	Summary of Events and Information	Remarks and references to Appendices
BERTRANCOURT	6.2.17		Routine sanitary inspections were made in the area. Further work was done in connection with getting the necessary information for a report on water supplies. Tracings were made from maps of the area and sketch plans of pumping stations, etc. Billet disinfection was carried out after a case of suspected C.S.M. in the 252nd R.E's at BERTUSSART. F. S. Carson, Capt. RAMCT	
BERTRANCOURT	7.2.17		I made a sanitary inspection of the village of MAILLY MAILLET and of the camps in MAILLY WOOD. I found that the sanitation was progressing very satisfactorily. Routine sanitary inspections were made in the area. I forwarded to the D.D.M.S. 5th Corps a complete report on the water supplies in my area accompanied by plans and maps. F. S. Carson, Capt. RAMCT	

A5834 Wt. W4973/M687 750,000 8/16 D. D. & L. Ltd. Forms/C.2113/13.

WAR DIARY or INTELLIGENCE SUMMARY.

(Erase heading not required.)

Army Form C. 2118.

Place	Date	Hour	Summary of Events and Information	Remarks and references to Appendices
BERTRANCOURT	8.2.17		I visited the village of VAUCHELLES and made a sanitary inspection of the area. I found that the sanitary condition was not improving. Water supplies in VAUCHELLES were re-tested. Routine sanitary inspections were made in the area. Disinfection of billets after cases of Dysentery were carried out at ACHEUX WOOD and "Y" Camp BERTRANCOURT. F.S. Carson Capt. RAMC	
BERTRANCOURT	9.2.17		I inspected the villages of BEAUSSART and MAILLY MAILLET and found the sanitary conditions generally good. The D.A.D.M.S (Sanitation) 5th Army called and inspected with me the village of BERTRANCOURT and camps in the vicinity, and the village of BEAUSSART. Routine sanitary inspections were continued.	

WAR DIARY
or
INTELLIGENCE SUMMARY.

(Erase heading not required.)

Army Form C. 2118.

Place	Date	Hour	Summary of Events and Information	Remarks and references to Appendices
BERTRANCOURT	10.2.17		Applied to the DDMS 6th Corps for the use of a motor cycle to enable me to make more frequent inspections in my area.	
			A.T. Cessou Capt. RAMC	
			Routine sanitary inspections were continued throughout the area.	
			The boring of water supplies in the area was continued. Arrangements were made for the discharge of the 9th (Hers) Pioneer Park to be circulated.	
			A.T. Cessou Capt. RAMC	
BERTRANCOURT	11.2.17		Inspected the village of Keueux in the afternoon and found that the sanitary condition was not so good as when I last inspected it.	
			Routine sanitary inspections were made in the area.	

Place	Date	Hour	Summary of Events and Information	Remarks and references to Appendices

BERTRANCOURT	12.2.17		Two huts in "Y" Camp BERTRANCOURT were disinfected after cases of Dysentery.
			
			            F. S. Carson Capt. RAMC
			
			 I inspected the camps in ACHEUX WOOD. I found several parts of the wood in a very untidy and insanitary condition.
			
			 Routine sanitary inspections were continued throughout the area.
			
			 Billets Nos 82 & 124 MAILLY MAILLET were disinfected after cases of Dysentery.
			
			            F. S. Carson Capt. RAMC.	

BERTRANCOURT	13.2.17		I made a sanitary inspection of BOLTON & LYTHAM Camps in MAILLY WOOD and found their condition satisfactory. I made suggestions regarding further accommodation in latrines to the	

Place	Date	Hour	Summary of Events and Information	Remarks and references to Appendices
BERTRANCOURT	14.7.17			

7.5 Cavan Cph RAMC

Camp Commandant asked to proceed to count and also inspected the camps in vicinity of BERTRANCOURT. Sanitary inspections were continued throughout the area.

7.6 Cavan Cph RAMC?

I inspected the villages of BERTRANCOURT and the Atelero also the village of MAILLY MAILLET, with special reference to water supplies. I invited the Town Commandants of these villages also examined a number of water carts, which were returning to the MAILLY MAILLET Stockyards, as regards their cleanness and efficiency of chlorination.

In the afternoon, I attended a Conference of Sanitary Officers at Corps Headquarters. Sanitary inspections were continued throughout the area.

7.5 Cavan Cph RAMC?

WAR DIARY
or
INTELLIGENCE SUMMARY.

(Erase heading not required.)

Army Form C. 2118.

Instructions regarding War Diaries and Intelligence Summaries are contained in F. S. Regs., Part II. and the Staff Manual respectively. Title pages will be prepared in manuscript.

Place	Date	Hour	Summary of Events and Information	Remarks and references to Appendices
BERTRANCOURT	15.2.17		In the morning I inspected the camps of units on the BERTRANCOURT — ACHEUX Road. In the afternoon I visited the village of LOUVENCOURT. Sanitary inspections were continued in the area including the village of BEAUSSART, 32nd DAC, 460 Coy. R.E. and 16th Siege Battery, R.G.A. A number of water carts were examined as to cleanliness and efficiency of chlorination when refilling at the new boring on the BERTRANCOURT — ACHEUX Road F.8a. F. S. Carson Cpl. S.F.M.O.	
BERTRANCOURT	16.2.17		I visited the village of VAUCHELLES and made a sanitary inspection accompanied by the Town Commandant. I found that the condition of the village was not improving. A list of the billets shewing insanitary conditions was handed	

WAR DIARY
or
INTELLIGENCE SUMMARY.

(Erase heading not required.)

Army Form C. 2118.

Place	Date	Hour	Summary of Events and Information	Remarks and references to Appendices
BERTENCOURT	17.2.17		At the Divn. Commandant's request of insanitary conditions existing in the villages of BERTENCOURT was handed to the Sous Commandant of the village. HEDAUVILLES and the Forward Area were inspected and found to be in a very insanitary condition.	
			A.S. Carson, Capt. D.A.D.C.	
			Inspected the A.S.C. lines and units on the BUS- BERTENCOURT Road. The camp of the 42.9 H.F.G. were found in an unsatisfactory condition and was reported. Routine sanitary inspection were continued. The week supplies of the forward area were again issued and tests made.	
			A.S. Carson, Capt. D.A.D.C.	

WAR DIARY or INTELLIGENCE SUMMARY.

(Erase heading not required.)

Army Form C. 2118.

Instructions regarding War Diaries and Intelligence Summaries are contained in F. S. Regs., Part II. and the Staff Manual respectively. Title pages will be prepared in manuscript.

Place	Date	Hour	Summary of Events and Information	Remarks and references to Appendices
BERTRANCOURT	8.2.17		I inspected the village of BERTRANCOURT and the camps in the vicinity and found that the condition was not improving owing to the lack of fatigue parties and of units constantly changing. In the afternoon I visited the ADMS 62nd Division. Sanitary inspections were continued throughout the area. F. S. Carson, Capt. RAMC	
BERTRANCOURT	9.2.17		In the morning I inspected the Headquarters Camp at BERTRANCOURT which was reported in a dirty condition owing to constant changing of units. Routine sanitary inspections were continued in the area. In the afternoon I visited the ADMS 7th Division. A Hut in "Z" Camp BERTRANCOURT was disinfected after a case of suspected Diphtheria. F. S. Carson, Capt. RAMC	

WAR DIARY
or
INTELLIGENCE SUMMARY.
(Erase heading not required.)

Army Form C. 2118.

Instructions regarding War Diaries and Intelligence Summaries are contained in F. S. Regs., Part II. and the Staff Manual respectively. Title pages will be prepared in manuscript.

Place	Date	Hour	Summary of Events and Information	Remarks and references to Appendices
BERTRANCOURT	20.2.17		I inspected the village and railhead at BEAUSSART and found the sanitation satisfactory. Routine sanitary inspections were continued in the area. The 5th Corps Siege Ammunition Park was inspected and found in an unsanitary condition.

F. S. Carson, Capt. RAMC | |
| BERTRANCOURT | 21.2.17 | | I inspected the village of MAILLY MAILLET in the morning. The sanitary condition was, as before, in a satisfactory condition. I also inspected a number of water carts, as to their cleanliness and efficiency of chlorination, at the standpipes at MAILLY MAILLET. Routine sanitary inspections in the area were continued | |

A5834 Wt. W4973/M687 750,000 8/16 D. D. & I. Ltd. Forms/C.2118/13.

WAR DIARY or INTELLIGENCE SUMMARY.

Army Form C. 2118.

(Erase heading not required.)

Place	Date	Hour	Summary of Events and Information	Remarks and references to Appendices
			In the evening I attended a Conference of Sanitary Officers at 7th Corps HQ. F. S. Carson. Capt. RAMC	
BERTRANCOURT	22.2.17		I inspected the forward area including FICHONVILLERS, WHITE CITY and BEAUMONT HAMEL with reference to the sanitation and water supply. I found that the sanitary condition of the forward area was unsatisfactory and was not improving. Sanitary inspections in the area were continued. The testing of water supplies in the area was continued. F. S. Carson. Capt. RAMC	
BERTRANCOURT	23.2.17		Sanitary inspections were made of the village of VAUCHELLES and the camps in MAILLY WOOD. The testing of water supplies and the routine	

WAR DIARY
or
INTELLIGENCE SUMMARY.

(Erase heading not required.)

Army Form C. 2118.

Instructions regarding War Diaries and Intelligence Summaries are contained in F. S. Regs., Part II. and the Staff Manual respectively. Title pages will be prepared in manuscript.

Place	Date	Hour	Summary of Events and Information	Remarks and references to Appendices
			Sanitary inspections were continued in the area. Sketch plans and maps were made to accompany the monthly sanitary Report. F. S. Carson Capt RAMC	
BERTRANCOURT	24.2.17		In the morning I drafted out my weekly and monthly Sanitary Reports on my area. Routine sanitary inspections and the testing and labelling of water supplies was continued. BOLTON and LYTHAM CAMPS _ MAILLY WOOD, were reported as having been left in a very insanitary condition F. S. Carson Capt RAMC	
BERTRANCOURT	28.2.17		I went to BEAUMONT HAMEL and the forward area with reference to the water supply of recently acquired territory. The ADMS together with a Corporal of my unit	

A5834   Wt. W4973/M687   750,000   8/16   D. D. & I. Ltd.   Forms/C.2113/13.

WAR DIARY
or
INTELLIGENCE SUMMARY.
(Erase heading not required.)

Army Form C. 2118.

Place	Date	Hour	Summary of Events and Information	Remarks and references to Appendices
			visited SERRE to investigate the water supply of this recently captured village and to test any wells in the village. Routine sanitary inspections were continued. I forwarded to the DDMS V Corps a Monthly Report on the sanitation in my area and of work completed, work in hand and work contemplated. This report was accompanied by plans of the villages in the area, a sketch plan shewing distribution of the personnel of my unit, a map of the water supply for the whole area and drawings of an incinerator in course of construction at BEAUSSART RAILHEAD for the drying up and burning of human excreta. F. S. Carson. Capt. RAMC	
BERTRANCOURT	26.2.17		I inspected the village of VAUCHELLES and found little progress in sanitation. Routine sanitary inspections were continued	

WAR DIARY
or
INTELLIGENCE SUMMARY.

(Erase heading not required.)

Place	Date	Hour	Summary of Events and Information	Remarks and references to Appendices
			Both No 8 BERTRANCOURT and Hut No 17 X camp BERTRANCOURT were disinfected after cases of MEASLES in the 8F Divison.	
			A.S. Cowan Capt RAMC	
BERTRANCOURT	2.7.17		I inspected a number of smoke cards in camp on the BERTRANCOURT - FRIERY ROAD. Items that little had been done to improve their sanitary condition since I last inspected them.	
			I also examined a number of water carts as regards their cleanliness and efficiency, at ACHEUX, at the new bath on the BERTRANCOURT - ACHEUX ROAD.	
			I sent to A.D.M.S. 4th Division and D.D.M.S. II Corps a short plan of BERTRANCOURT HAMEL showing positions of workplaces, new private deep trench latrine.	
			Routine Sanitary inspections were continued	
			A.S. Cowan Capt RAMC	

Army Form C. 2118.

WAR DIARY or INTELLIGENCE SUMMARY

Army Form C. 2118.

Instructions regarding War Diaries and Intelligence Summaries are contained in F. S. Regs., Part II. and the Staff Manual respectively. Title pages will be prepared in manuscript.

(Erase heading not required.)

Place	Date	Hour	Summary of Events and Information	Remarks and references to Appendices
BERTRANCOURT	28.2.17		I inspected the 62nd Divisional Ammunition Column in camp on the FIENVILLERS – BERTRANCOURT Road. I found that no improvement had been made on the sanitary condition as I last found it. I made a number of suggestions to the CO for the improvement of the camps. Routine sanitary inspections were carried out in the area. The testing of water supplies and examination of water carts were continued in the area. Two NCOs were sent to the dressing station at RED HOUSE MAILLY MAILLET to test the water supplies in PUISIEUX and other recently captured territory.	Capt R.H.M.G F. S. Carson.

No. 10 SECTION
2ND LONDON SANITARY COY R.A.M.C.T
B.E. FORCE. FRANCE.

Mar. 1917

WAR DIARY
FROM 1ST MARCH TO 31ST MARCH 1917
Vol: 8.

CONFIDENTIAL.

14/2043

COMMITTEE FOR THE
MEDICAL HISTORY OF THE WAR.
Date 11 MAY 1917

Vol 8
10 Sanitary Section

WAR DIARY
or
INTELLIGENCE SUMMARY.

(Erase heading not required.)

Army Form C. 2118.

Instructions regarding War Diaries and Intelligence Summaries are contained in F. S. Regs., Part II. and the Staff Manual respectively. Title pages will be prepared in manuscript.

Place	Date	Hour	Summary of Events and Information	Remarks and references to Appendices
BERTRANCOURT	1.3.17		I went to SERRE and PUISIEUX (recently taken from the enemy) to obtain samples of water from wells, for the purpose of testing for poisons and to ascertain whether the water was potable. Three samples were obtained in the village of PUISIEUX. Twelve men from the 4th Division reported for water guard duties in the area. Disinfection was carried out after a case of measles in the 9/Cheshires at BOUCHELLES and three cases of Scarlet Fever in ACHEUX WOOD. F. S. Carson, Capt. RAMC	
BERTRANCOURT	2.3.17		I tested the samples of water obtained from wells in PUISIEUX. In each case the water was found to be poison-free and that for chlorination, one scoop of bleaching powder was required per water cart.	

WAR DIARY
or
INTELLIGENCE SUMMARY

Army Form C. 2118.

Place	Date	Hour	Summary of Events and Information	Remarks and references to Appendices
BERTRANCOURT	23.17		Routine sanitary inspections in the area were continued. Disinfection was carried out after five cases of Measles in the Depots at the BERNERY – NEUILLY MAILLET.	
			4.5 Canadian Casualty Adrmct.	
			The DADMS. i/c Division called in the morning 13th. Reference is the Infectious Diseases of the Divisions and as to the sanitary condition of the Camps in ACHEUX Wood. In the afternoon I inspected BOLTON Camp. Scale plans of HICKONVILLERS were sent to the DDMS. Taps over RDMS of Division showing the positions of proposed new deep trench public latrines. Disinfection was carried out after a case of Diphtheria at HERIEUX, also further cases of Measles in Depots at NEUILLY MAILLET and a case of Measles in the Depots.	
			4.5 Canadian Capt. Ramsey.	

Place	Date	Hour	Summary of Events and Information	Remarks and references to Appendices
BERTRANCOURT	4.3.17		I inspected the camps in MAILLY WOOD, and found that the sanitary condition was not improving. They were very untidy.	
			Routine sanitary inspections in the area were continued	
			Disinfection was carried out after a case of measles in the Border Regt. and one in the Devon's both at MAILLY MAILLET.	
			F. S. Carson, Capt. RAMC	
BERTRANCOURT	5.3.17		I inspected the village of BERTRANCOURT and the camps in the vicinity of the village. The area vacated by the 62nd Divisional Ammunition Column on the ACHEUX ROAD at R3c. was found in an unsatisfactory condition and six dead horses were left unburied. These conditions were reported.	
			Sketch plans of ACHONVILLERS and BEAUMONT HAMEL	

WAR DIARY
or
INTELLIGENCE SUMMARY.

(Erase heading not required.)

Instructions regarding War Diaries and Intelligence Summaries are contained in F. S. Regs., Part II. and the Staff Manual respectively. Title pages will be prepared in manuscript.

Army Form C. 2118.

Place	Date	Hour	Summary of Events and Information	Remarks and references to Appendices
			shewing the positions of proposed new public latrines, were sent to the Town Major at "Y" RAVINE	
			The water guard men, who were now trained in their duties, were posted to the various water cart refilling points in the area.	
			Disinfection was carried out after a case of Measles in the 3HAC at "Y" CAMP.	
			7. S. Carson, Capt. RAMCT.	
BERTRANCOURT	6·3·17		In the morning I inspected BOLTON and LYTHAM CAMPS, MAILLY WOOD. BOLTON CAMP had been cleared up considerably by the unit in occupation — 2Queens (Royal West Surrey Regt). Much improvement was required in LYTHAM CAMP as regards provision of latrine.	
			A NCO of this Section was attached to the Town Major of BEAUMONT HAMEL to inspect and prepare schemes	

A5834 Wt. W4973/M687 750,000 8/16 D. D. & I. Ltd. Forms/C.2118/13.

WAR DIARY
or
INTELLIGENCE SUMMARY.

(Erase heading not required.)

Army Form C. 2118.

Instructions regarding War Diaries and Intelligence Summaries are contained in F. S. Regs., Part II. and the Staff Manual respectively. Title pages will be prepared in manuscript.

Place	Date	Hour	Summary of Events and Information	Remarks and references to Appendices
			for the sanitation of BEAUMONT HAMEL, WHITE CITY and BEAUCOURT. The testing and labelling of water supplies was carried out at MAILLY MAILLY, FLUCHONVILLERS and BEAUMONT HAMEL. Routine sanitary inspections were made in the area. F. G. Carson, Capt. RAMC	
BERTRANCOURT	7-3-17		I inspected the village of BERTRANCOURT and the surrounding camps and found that much improvement was necessary in their sanitary condition. In the afternoon I attended a Conference of Sanitary Officers at V Corps HQ. A general inspection of BEAUCOURT, MIRAUMONT and the forward area recently captured from the enemy was made. Water supplies were found at BEAUCOURT and MIRAUMONT. These were tested and found to be free from metallic poisons and	

WAR DIARY
or
INTELLIGENCE SUMMARY.

(Erase heading not required.)

Place	Date	Hour	Summary of Events and Information	Remarks and references to Appendices
BETRANCOURT			men inspected accordingly. Disinfection was carried out at FIENVILLERS after a case of infectious disease in the South Wales Borderers.	
		4.5	Owners Capt. Barker	
			The A.D.M.S. Divison asked to see no work reference to the erection of temporary latrines on ground recently captured from the enemy. On it was found that trenches are still here near the roads were fenced with wire. In the afternoon I visited VAUCHELLES. It is/not a summer hut camp. This camp consisted of eight wooden huts without doors. Its fort because once huts were in most of the huts had been demolished. Accomodation for presumably reported that the camp was unfit for habitation by troops.	

Place	Date	Hour	Summary of Events and Information	Remarks and references to Appendices
			Routine sanitary inspections were carried out throughout the area.	
			Disinfection was carried out after two cases of measles in the 7th D.A.C.	
			F. S. Carson, Capt. R.A.M.C.	
BERTRANCOURT	9.3.17		I inspected the camps at MAILLY WOOD and the village of BEAUSSART. The former camps I found in a good sanitary condition. At BEAUSSART I found that the area vacated by the 62nd Divisional Artillery had been left in an unsanitary condition and reported accordingly.	
			A scheme was prepared to deal with the waste water from a laundry and bath house, for a rest station, under construction at VAUCHELLES, by the bleaching powder method of clarification. A NCO of this Section was sent to supervise the work.	

WAR DIARY
or
INTELLIGENCE SUMMARY.

(Erase heading not required.)

Instructions regarding War Diaries and Intelligence Summaries are contained in F. S. Regs., Part II. and the Staff Manual respectively. Title pages will be prepared in manuscript.

Army Form C. 2118.

Place	Date	Hour	Summary of Events and Information	Remarks and references to Appendices
			Disinfections were carried out after cases of measles in the Northumberland Yeomanry at I Corps HQ and in the 2/5 W. Riding Battalion at Mailly.	
			F. S. Carson, Capt. RAMC	
BERTRANCOURT	31		I inspected the villages of BEAUSSART and MAILLY MAILLET. In both cases I found these villages in a good sanitary condition. In MAILLY MAILLET the erection of latrines and incinerators for the whole village was nearly completed.	
			A N.C.O was sent to the 7th Divisional Gas School at VAUCHELLES for further training in gas precautions.	
			Disinfections were carried out after cases of Scarlet Fever at ACHEUX and Measles in the 4Q.O Hussars at ACHEUX.	
			F. S. Carson, Capt. RAMC	

A5834 Wt. W4973/M687 750,000 8/16 D. D. & L. Ltd. Forms/C.2118/13.

WAR DIARY
or
INTELLIGENCE SUMMARY.

(Erase heading not required.)

Army Form C. 2118.

Instructions regarding War Diaries and Intelligence Summaries are contained in F. S. Regs., Part II. and the Staff Manual respectively. Title pages will be prepared in manuscript.

Place	Date	Hour	Summary of Events and Information	Remarks and references to Appendices
BERTRANCOURT	11-3-17		I inspected the camps outside BEAUSSART (P.9a) and the 7th Divisional Ammunition Column. Routine Sanitary inspections were made in the area. Disinfection was carried out after a case of Measles in the 2HAC at LYNDHURST CAMP. F. S. Carson, Capt. D.M.T	
BERTRANCOURT	12-3-17		In the morning I inspected the village of VAUCHELLES. Although, owing to the shortage of materials and skilled labour, no further constructional work had been done, the village was much cleaner than when I had visited it. Disinfections were carried out after a case of Scarlet Fever in the 2Queen's at Y Camp, and a case of Dysentery in the 2Gordons at Bertrancourt. F. S. Carson, Capt. D.M.T	

WAR DIARY
or
INTELLIGENCE SUMMARY.

(Erase heading not required.)

Army Form C. 2118.

Instructions regarding War Diaries and Intelligence Summaries are contained in F. S. Regs., Part II. and the Staff Manual respectively. Title pages will be prepared in manuscript.

Place	Date	Hour	Summary of Events and Information	Remarks and references to Appendices
BERTRANCOURT	13.3.17		Inspected the villages of BEAUSSART, MAILLY MAILLET and FLUCHONVILLERS.	
			Routine Sanitary inspections were carried out in the area	
			Disinfection was carried out after a case of measles in the H.A.C. at Lyndhurst Camp - BERTRANCOURT	
			F. S. Carson, Capt. R.A.M.C.	
BERTRANCOURT	14.3.17		Inspected the village of BERTRANCOURT and to surrounding camps. In the afternoon I attended a Conference of Sanitary Officers at V Corps H.Q.	
			Two NCOs were sent to RED HOUSE in the forward area (near MIRAUX) for water duties in territory recently captured from the enemy.	
			Disinfections were carried out after cases of	

A5834 Wt. W4973/M687 750,000 8/16 D. D. & L. Ltd. Forms/C.2118/13.

WAR DIARY or INTELLIGENCE SUMMARY.

Army Form C. 2118.

Place	Date	Hour	Summary of Events and Information	Remarks and references to Appendices
			Measles in the Royal Munster Fusiliers at FIENEUX, H.A.C. at Lyndhurst Camp, BERTRANCOURT and the 7 Signal Coy at BEAUSSART. F. S. Carson, Capt. R.A.M.C.	
BERTRANCOURT	15.3.17		Having been running a temperature for the last twelve hours I remained off duty after notifying the DDMS I Corps and ADMS 7th Division. Routine sanitary inspections were continued throughout the area. Disinfections were carried out after cases of Measles at the Church Army Hut BERTRANCOURT, 2nd Manchesters, 2 Gordons, 2HAC and 20 Manchesters. F. S. Carson, Capt. R.A.M.C.	
BERTRANCOURT	16.3.17		I remained off duty to-day.	

WAR DIARY
or
INTELLIGENCE SUMMARY.

(Erase heading not required.)

Instructions regarding War Diaries and Intelligence Summaries are contained in F. S. Regs., Part II. and the Staff Manual respectively. Title pages will be prepared in manuscript.

Army Form C. 2118.

Place	Date	Hour	Summary of Events and Information	Remarks and references to Appendices
			Routine Sanitary inspections were made in the area. Disinfections were carried out after cases of measles in the Devons at MAILLY. F. S. Carson, Capt. RAMC	
BERTRANCOURT	17.3.17		Routine Sanitary inspections were made in the area. Water carts were examined as to their cleanliness and efficiency of chlorination while refilling at MAILLY and the boring on the BERTRANCOURT–ACHEUX Road. In all cases the water was found to be chlorinated. Disinfection was carried out after a case of Measles at MAILLY (Devons) F. S. Carson, Capt. RAMC	
BERTRANCOURT	18.3.17		A NCO was attached to the 23rd Field Ambulance	

A5834   Wt. W4973/M687   750,000   8/16   D. D. & L. Ltd.   Forms/C.2118/13.

WAR DIARY or INTELLIGENCE SUMMARY.

(Erase heading not required.)

Army Form C. 2118.

Place	Date	Hour	Summary of Events and Information	Remarks and references to Appendices
			to make further tests of water supplies on captured territory. Routine Sanitary inspections were carried out in the area Disinfection was carried out after a case of measles at the 31 Divisional School at VAUCHELLES. F. S. Carson Capt. RAMC	
BERTRANCOURT	9.3.17		Sanitary inspections were carried out in the forward area of BEAUCOURT, MIRAUMONT and IRLES. Samples of water were taken from these villages for testing Sanitary inspections were also made at ACHEUX and camps on the BERTRANCOURT – ACHEUX ROAD. Disinfections were carried out after cases of measles at the 1 Divisional School and the 2 Borders and Devons at MAILLY MAILLET. F. S. Carson. Capt. RAMC	

WAR DIARY
or
INTELLIGENCE SUMMARY.

Army Form C. 2118.

Place	Date	Hour	Summary of Events and Information	Remarks and references to Appendices
BERTRANCOURT	20.3.17		Inspected the village of BERTRANCOURT and the camps in the vicinity of the village. There were no troops in most of the camps. Found the villages in a much cleaner condition than when I last inspected. Routine sanitary inspections were made throughout the area. Disinfection was carried out after a case of measles in the Officers at MAILLY MAILLET. ‡ S. Canan, Capt. R.A.M.C.	
BERTRANCOURT	21.3.17		Further inspections were made in the forenoon. Routine sanitary inspections were continued. Disinfection was carried out after a case of Enteric Pyrexia in the 23 Manchester. ‡ S. Canan, Capt. R.A.M.C.	

WAR DIARY or INTELLIGENCE SUMMARY.

Army Form C. 2118.

(Erase heading not required.)

Place	Date	Hour	Summary of Events and Information	Remarks and references to Appendices
BERTRANCOURT	22.3.17		I inspected the camps in Mailly Wood and the village of MAILLY MAILLET. The camps, which were practically empty of troops, were in a good sanitary condition. The village also was very satisfactory. Public Latrines and incinerators for the whole village were completed with large notice boards shewing their positions. I also inspected a number of water carts which were refilling at the standpipes at MAILLY. Routine sanitary inspections were made throughout the area. F. S. Carson, Capt. R.A.M.C.	
BERTRANCOURT	23.3.17		O.C. No 7 Sanitary Section called in the morning with reference to taking over from me the sanitary supervision of the villages of VAUCHELLES	

WAR DIARY
or
INTELLIGENCE SUMMARY.

(Erase heading not required.)

Army Form C. 2118.

Instructions regarding War Diaries and Intelligence Summaries are contained in F. S. Regs., Part II. and the Staff Manual respectively. Title pages will be prepared in manuscript.

Place	Date	Hour	Summary of Events and Information	Remarks and references to Appendices
			LOUVENCOURT and FICHEUX. I arranged to leave the N.C.Os of my Section, who were attached to the Town Majors of these villages, to hand over and give any information to the N.C.Os of No 71 Sanitary Section. I also handed over to the OC No 71 Sanitary Section sketch plans of these villages shewing the schemes of sanitation also papers relating to their water supplies. Disinfection was carried out after a case of measles in the 8Devons. F. S. Carson, Capt. R.A.M.C.	
BERTRANCOURT	24·3·17		Routine sanitary inspections were made throughout the area. Disinfection was carried out after a case of measles in the 528 Coy, RE, at BEAUSSART. F. S. Carson, Capt. R.A.M.C.	

A5834   Wt. W4973/M687   750,000   8/16   D. D. & L. Ltd.   Forms/C.2118/13.

WAR DIARY or INTELLIGENCE SUMMARY

Army Form C. 2118.

(Erase heading not required.)

Instructions regarding War Diaries and Intelligence Summaries are contained in F. S. Regs., Part II. and the Staff Manual respectively. Title pages will be prepared in manuscript.

Place	Date	Hour	Summary of Events and Information	Remarks and references to Appendices
BERTRANCOURT	25.3.17		The villages of VAUCHELLES, LOUVENCOURT and FIENEUX were now taken over from me by O.C. No 71 Sanitary Section. The NCO's of this section were withdrawn from these villages. Routine sanitary inspections were made throughout the area. F. S. Carron, Capt. R.A.M.C.	
BERTRANCOURT	26.3.17		I inspected the village and roadhead at BEAUSSART. I found that general sanitation was being much neglected and no fatigue parties were being obtained by the Town Major. Constructional work was at a standstill. The area vacated by the 91st Brigade Transport was left in a dirty condition. I reported these to the D.D.M.S. V Corps and to the A.D.M.S. 7th Division. Routine sanitary inspections were made in the area. F. S. Carron, Capt. R.A.M.C.	

WAR DIARY
-or-
INTELLIGENCE SUMMARY.

(Erase heading not required.)

Army Form C. 2118.

Instructions regarding War Diaries and Intelligence Summaries are contained in F. S. Regs., Part II. and the Staff Manual respectively. Title pages will be prepared in manuscript.

Place	Date	Hour	Summary of Events and Information	Remarks and references to Appendices
BERTRANCOURT	27.3.17		I received orders from the I Corps to move the Headquarters of this Section from BERTRANCOURT to MIRAUMONT. I went to MIRAUMONT to find a suitable place to fix the camp. The motor lorry with tents etc. moved to MIRAUMONT in the afternoon. Water carts were examined as regards their cleanliness and efficiency of chlorination. Water Supplies at MIRAUMONT were tested. F. S. Cannon Capt. RAMC	
MIRAUMONT	28.3.17		The Headquarters of this Section moved into camp at MIRAUMONT L35c 4.9. Sheet 57d Two NCO's were left behind and attached to the Town Major of BERTRANCOURT to supervise the sanitation of that village and the village and Railhead of BEAUSSART.	

A5834   Wt. W4973/M687   750,000   8/16   D. D. & L. Ltd.   Form-/C.2113/13.

WAR DIARY
or
INTELLIGENCE SUMMARY.

(Erase heading not required.)

Army Form C. 2118.

Instructions regarding War Diaries and Intelligence Summaries are contained in F. S. Regs., Part II. and the Staff Manual respectively. Title pages will be prepared in manuscript.

Place	Date	Hour	Summary of Events and Information	Remarks and references to Appendices
			I attended a conference of sanitary officers at I Corps HQ in the afternoon. The villages of ACHIET-LE-PETIT, ERVILLERS and St LEGER were allotted to this Section for Sanitary Supervision. F. S. Carson, Capt. R.A.M.C.	
MIRAUMONT	29.3.17		I received a notification from I Corps H.Q. that during the absence of O.C. No. 21 Sanitary Section, I would supervise the area of that Section in addition to my own. Routine sanitary inspections were made throughout the area. F. S. Carson Capt. R.A.M.C.	
MIRAUMONT	30.3.17		I inspected the village of MIRAUMONT and found that it was in an unsanitary condition. Excreta	

WAR DIARY
or
INTELLIGENCE SUMMARY.
(Erase heading not required.)

Army Form C. 2118.

Instructions regarding War Diaries and Intelligence Summaries are contained in F. S. Regs., Part II. and the Staff Manual respectively. Title pages will be prepared in manuscript.

Place	Date	Hour	Summary of Events and Information	Remarks and references to Appendices
			was found in nearly every shell hole and inside dilapidated buildings.	
			Routine sanitary inspections were continued	
			F. S. Carson Capt. R.A.M.C	
MIRAUMONT	31.3.17		I inspected the villages of ACHIET-LE-PETIT. Water supplies were found and tested in ACHIET-LE-PETIT, ERVILLERS and S.T LEGER. In no case was the water found to be poisoned.	
			A sanitary inspection of ERVILLERS and S.T LEGER shewed that there were practically no sanitary arrangements in use. The area generally was found in a clean condition.	
			F. S. Carson, Capt. R.A.M.C	

A5834 Wt. W4973/M687 750,000 8/16 D. D. & L. Ltd. Forms/C.2118/13.